A son of Bayeux

Rannulf 'Flambard'

1060-1128

The true story of his eventful career in Norman England

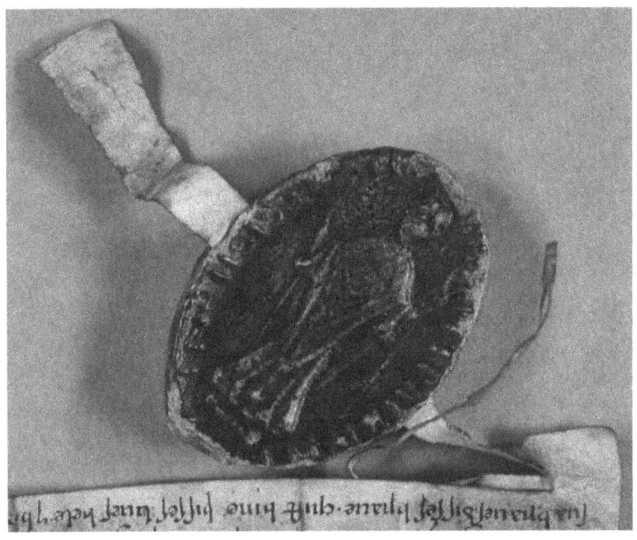

Sally Harvey
&
Gordon Sawyer

 A catalogue record for this book is available from the National Library of Australia

Copyright © 2024 Gordon Sawyer
All rights reserved.
ISBN-13: 978-1-923174-26-9

Linellen Press
265 Boomerang Road
Oldbury, Western Australia
www.linellenpress.com.au

The Making of This Book

The idea for this book came from Doctor Sally Harvey. For half a century, Sally, an academic historian, had been a lecturer and researcher in history at the universities of Cambridge, Leeds and Oxford. Her special interests were the Norman Conquest and Domesday. Her book, *Domesday, Book of Judgement* is widely considered by her peers to be 'a major contribution to Domesday scholarship'.

Rannulf, nicknamed Flambard, rose to prominence during the reign of William II, Rufus, but, until recently, his reputation had been tainted through the writings of chroniclers of the day because of his close association with the fiscal policies of Rufus much despised by church leaders and barons alike. As a consequence, his many positive and lasting achievements had been overlooked for centuries. Even today, he is probably most well known for being the first person to be imprisoned in the Tower of London and the first to escape!

But as 20th-century researchers began to explore this period in our history more, Rannulf's achievements began to be reevaluated. Sally found him a fascinating character. She liked the rascal element in his character, which no doubt led to his nickname, Flambard. She admired his willingness to take on Archbishop Anselm's might, the risks he took, and his guile.

Having retired from academia, Sally decided to tell the story of his life, not as a piece of academic research, but rather as a story. Rannulf's work, his achievements, his mistakes, and even some of the scandals attributed to him are well recorded though rarely have seen the light of day save to the academic historians of Medieval England. This book is designed to help put that right!

Little is known, however, of his family and his private life. Illuminating these gaps was important for Sally as they help us understand the values that shaped many of Rannulf's decisions and, perhaps, how he was able to leapfrog his more academically and socially gifted contemporaries. She used her knowledge of the period to imagine these parts of the story, most notably his upbringing in Bayeux. They are written in an immersive style, often using speech, and will be easily recognisable to the reader.

Her aim has been to shed light on Rannulf's unique rise from humble beginnings to top man under Rufus and the lasting legacy he left in Durham, where he was Prince Bishop of Durham from 1099 to his death there in 1128. It is hoped that the story of this most remarkable man will be of interest to people of all ages who are interested in history, whether students at school or college or, more broadly, by how our past has shaped our present.

Although Sally had completed her research for the book and had made a good start in writing the text, her health prevented her from completing it. She shared her passion for the project as well as her frustration at not being able to finish it with me, a neighbour where she now lives in Great Malvern. As someone who has an interest in local history and has already written a local history book, I was intrigued. After reading her texts and notes, and with my own online research, I too became enthused with Rannulf's story and volunteered, with much trepidation, to complete the book.

Sally had been in two minds about including much historical context, but I felt it had to be included. That background best explains not just what Rannulf did but how and why his career took its many twists and turns. The final book not only documents the life of a most remarkable, largely unknown person but also provides a springboard for the reader to delve into other aspects of how the Norman Conquest shaped England's history.

Towards the end of my work, I decided to contact the Durham Cathedral Library. Imogen Conroy, library services officer, responded. Her enthusiastic and fulsome responses helped me enormously in validating and deepening my research via Wikipedia and understanding Sally's knowledge, which, sadly, I could not tap into.

Enjoy the read!

Gordon Sawyer,
Great Malvern
May 2024

List of Illustrations

Chapter 3

Bishop Odo surrendering at Rochester Castle. Photo by Patrick Gray by kind permission of Flickr Pro and Creative Commons

Christchurch Priory 900th anniversary sculpture. Photo by Elliot Brown by kind permission of Flickr Pro and Creative Commons

Bishop Rannulf's seal. Reproduced by kind permission of the Chapter of Durham Cathedral

Chapter 7

Site plan of Durham Peninsular. By kind permission of Durham World Heritage Centre

Durham Cathedral sanctuary door knocker. Photo by Michael Beckwith by kind permission of Flickr and Creative Commons

Chapter 8

Durham Cathedral Chapter House. Photo by kind permission of the Chapter of Durham Cathedral

Contents

The Making of This Book 1
Contents 5
Introduction 7
Chapter 1 - Growing up in Bayeux 11
Chapter 2 - Life under William the Conqueror 38
Chapter 3 - England under William Rufus 53
Chapter 4 - Escape to Normandy 71
Chapter 5 - Life back in Normandy 88
Chapter 6 - Time to Leave 105
Chapter 7 - Prince Bishop of Durham 118
Chapter 8 - The End 136
References and further reading 144
About the Authors 145

Introduction

Although it is impossible to predict the course of our lives, the environment in which we grew up undoubtedly plays a major part: family, place, and time. And so it was with Rannulf.

Rannulf was born in Bayeux, Normandy, just a few years before Duke William of Normandy set out in 1066 to conquer England. He was one of four brothers; he also had a younger sister. His father was a priest, Thurstin, a member of the chapter of Bayeux Cathedral. His grandfather was a rural priest in a village just a horse ride away. The Bishop of Bayeux was the charismatic Odo, half-brother of Duke William and his right-hand man at the Battle of Hastings. He was more soldier than bishop, but a man who also founded the cathedral school, built Bayeux's new cathedral, and who commissioned the Bayeux Tapestry that would be hung in the new cathedral when it was inaugurated in 1077.

As Rannulf grew into his teens, he watched with fascination the comings and goings between the town and its port, Port-en-Bessin, just a few kilometres to the north; horses, equipment and soldiers going out and the spoils of the conquerors coming in. He often saw Odo in his fine robes atop his mighty horse parading with his soldiers. Odo was a hero figure not just to Rannulf but to many in the town. Not surprisingly, the teenage Rannulf developed a yearning to go to England to discover what this new kingdom just across the Channel was really like.

His moral compass throughout his life was set by his family, especially his father and grandfather. He disliked war; he knew he did not want to be a soldier and always believed there had to be a better way than war to resolve disputes. He developed a good understanding of the lives of the peasant farmer and the unfair treatment they often received from greedy landowners. But, as a canon's son, he was fortunate to be taught at the cathedral school. He wasn't academically bright, particularly in Latin or the Arts, which meant he would never get to the top school at Liege, for example, necessary if you wanted to progress rapidly in the Church hierarchy. He preferred to skip lessons and spend time in the stables where he learnt much about horses and horsemanship. In his teens, he was appointed to minor orders in the cathedral and accompanied Odo and officials of the bishopric on missions to church estates and other dioceses. The skills he developed set him on a different course from most of his peers at school.

This book tells Rannulf's story, a true story, though some parts, such as his early years in Bayeux, are imagined based on the known facts of the period. It sets out to explain how Rannulf got his first break to go to England and how he seized opportunities that came his way leading him to the very top of the administration of William Rufus, the Conqueror's second son and his successor as King of England. It tells how he became appointed by Rufus as Prince Bishop of Durham but shortly thereafter imprisoned in the Tower of London by King Henry. It tells of his reinstatement at Durham and the defences he conceived and built, which have stood the test of time, shaping the World Heritage site there today.

Many of the chroniclers of the time wrote scathingly of Rannulf, largely because of his role in implementing the money raising schemes of his boss, Rufus, which were much hated by church leaders and barons alike. Indeed, the Archbishop of

Canterbury, Anselm, no friend of Rannulf, spoke ill of him to the Pope, describing him as 'almost illiterate' and when asked why Rannulf's nickname was Flambard, replied 'because he was cruel, like a flaming torch'.

The 1971 Cathedral Lecture given by H S Offler, Professor of Medieval History at Durham University, entitled 'Rannulf Flambard as Bishop of Durham' quoted the renowned Oxford historian Sir Richard Southern. Southern described Rannulf's role under King William II, Rufus, as the King's "chief legal and financial expert". He also described Rannulf as "The first outstandingly successful administrator in English history. This son of an obscure priest in the diocese of Bayeux was the first man of ignoble birth in English history to climb from the bottom to the top of the social scale by the backstairs of the royal administration".

But perhaps the last words should belong to a monk of Durham, who knew Rannulf, writing after his death, 'that was our golden age under Rannulf our bishop'.

The story of this most remarkable man begins on his first day at school in Bayeux in the winter following the Battle of Hastings.

Chapter 1

Growing up in Bayeux

The small boy awoke cold and shivering. Dim starlight from slits of windows high in the draughty barn-like building slowly revealed outlines of other boys asleep on their straw pallets: no disturbing dream this, but his new life.

He lay unaccountably stiff and straight. Last night, his first night here, he had managed to warm himself by endlessly wriggling; it had proved effective. Slightly comforted, he had made himself re-live a few of the reasons why he must make the most of this new step. Then, tiring again with the effort of visualising unknown possibilities, their opportunities and their dangers, and still longing for the little cupboard recess that he had always shared with his younger sister in the low-ceilinged room at home, he had pretended that he was back with her on the old sawdust mattress by wrapping his long thin arms around himself, imagining they were hers, and, curling up, had slept.

But tonight, his second night, he could not warm himself like that. No longer master of his own sleeping place, he felt all the more isolated and desolate for that. He had been assigned to a different pallet and told to lie on it head to tail with an older boy whom he had been instructed by no means to disturb. The senior boy, full of confidence and, with a touch of the bully, had reinforced the instruction. 'Let a hand or foot touch me, and you'll be thrashed ... and in the morning you'll be reported to the

Master of the School and thrashed again ... and made to live separately from the rest of us.'

So now, on the shivering boy's second night, he missed not only the close breathing of his small sister, he missed the whole smoky warmth of home: especially his mother: her almost complicit smile at his cheekiness, her still-bright eyes, and the good thick smells of cooking on her clothing. He wanted to give in, give up, and, something he, as the eldest, had not allowed himself to do for a couple of years now, he wanted to sob. But then, after cautiously wriggling first one foot a little and then the other, he managed to force himself to think again of his hopes and his purposes: not only the full day in school he had just got through with certain credit if no great merit, albeit with not inconsiderable effort. The aim, the central thing, was the strong chance he would have, once schooled, to join the household of the young bishop.

The boy had often hung about for hours outside the cathedral when the bishop was expected in the town. The exuberant and youthful bishop, who for some years now had official care of all the souls in the diocese of Bayeux, was neither a theologian nor a man of the mind nor a man of peace. He was far more given to worldly affairs than spiritual contemplation: always worth watching, either at the culmination of a religious procession or in armour at the head of a group of young knights. A man of action, and of restless ambition, it was hard to see how life could offer him much more. Already by the grace of his half-brother, he was one of the very highest in the dukedom and bishop of a rich diocese. Common gossip held that Bishop Odo was a cleric in name only since outside the precincts of his own cathedral, he was usually surrounded by secular companions: all young knights, very evidently relishing their own fine armour, horses, and dress. It was often difficult to single out the one or two young clerics in his entourage as they too, when they could get hold of them, rode horses of quality alongside the knights. But, whether in episcopal cloak or in chain mail, Odo was always easy to pick out. Whatever place he filled in a formal procession, or amongst the faster-moving and forceful clatter of well-shod hooves, his silver-grey mounts stood out from all others. Their distinguishing colour apart, his mounts had a delicacy and refinement that the knowledgeable rarely saw but whose flowing action they appreciated when they did.

The Norman duchy was known for its rich pasture and its sturdy, capable horses; but the bishop's horses were no horses of Normandy. His mounts had been purchased directly from Spain and, it was told, had been bred from famous horses brought from somewhere near the holy city of Jerusalem; certainly from lands beyond the Mediterranean Sea. But the bishop was not simply an interloper into high ecclesiastical office by accident of birth. His determined ambitions had always included the Church of Bayeux and the foundation there of a new great cathedral, first planned by his predecessor in 1044, with funds ready and waiting, albeit many from unrecognised and unacknowledged sources. Deep excavations now awaiting the new crypt were disturbing the once-ordered life in the vicinity of the Cathedral.

Despite the mud and chaos surrounding the new construction, the school attached to the old cathedral when first established was now known to be offering one of the best avenues to advancement, attracting not just the attention of the chapter clergy for their own sons and the wealthier clergy of the diocese for their sons; its reputation meant it recruited widely from landowning families, and several of the more locally alert families.

Like everyone else in Normandy, the small boy knew why. It was not solely the quality of education: that at Caen, Bec, Rouen and the schools of France and the Empire were most probably superior. It was all because their bishop, Odo, was privy to and central to decisions – some made in this very group of buildings, even instrumental to the great events ensuing. Decisions so fantastical almost to be beyond belief and whose effects reverberated across the whole of Normandy, and beyond. Terrifying decisions, if only half the say-so is believed, for the kingdom of England across the Channel, where chaos now reigned, yet where Duke William and his half-brother, the very Bishop Odo known here in Bayeux since his ordination in 1047, were said now to rule and command. No end of tales continually circulated in the town and the surrounding countryside and riverside – and it became harder by the day to begin to distinguish fact from fantasy. It was told how the brothers' new lands boasted ancient monasteries stacked with golden treasures; certainly the ship-workers in Bayeux's port, Port-en-Bessin some seven kilometres north, had direct experience of the chests of treasures that were being brought back by the boat-load to fill the sanctuaries of some newly-founded monasteries here in Normandy and certainly the immediate reality was that there was no difficulty in re-building the cathedral from the proceeds.

The boy, called Rannulf, yearned to have a part in such great happenings, but there was a questioning besides. Did all that he'd heard, in fact, amount to stealing? Had, or would, God bless the enterprise? Was it theft if some profits went to a sacred cause here, to a reconstruction of the revered Church of Bayeux, which was the very focus of the town and the source of trade and prosperity in all the countryside around?

Some did say that, despite all the sacred buildings and ceremonies here in Bayeux, the outcome would be dire as and when God made his judgement known. Certainly, some of the treasures arriving daily were looted. That theft was wrong was something his father and mother had always put great efforts to instill in their eldest boy, and all of his grandfather's way of life was governed by this principle. Had they not instructed him to avoid the escapades that he had so enjoyed with the other boys when they slipped out of town at dusk to jump on the backs of the traders' ponies in the town fields, and when they scrumped apples and even vegetables from the small plots hand-dug by the market holders beneath the city walls? His parents had impressed upon him that these gardening men and women, the local horticulturalists, had an unremitting task to get crops from under the town walls to feed their own labouring families, let alone enough to sell some fresh produce to the inhabitants in the town market to provide their working boots and corn for their daily bread. Whereas Rannulf's own father, Thirstin, as a canon of the cathedral, seldom encountered poor rations for his family except when a hard winter denied supplies to almost everyone. Even then his family usually had access to a grain supply stored on some estate under the Church of Bayeux's control.

That, of course, did not mean that Rannulf had always followed his parents' precepts, especially when they didn't seem to apply to him. He now avoided taking any vegetables from the small allotments, but he loved to join his comrades when they went jumping on the ponies' bare backs and attempting to ride them, especially so because he was better at it than most; he loved to show off, teasing, even gloating over those of his fellows who fell off more often than he did. But recently, he had worked out that it was probably safer to do that on his own; it was less likely that he would be noticed, or that his companions might, inadvertently perhaps, tell their elders. So now he took these illicit ventures by himself, without saddle or reins, using only the horse's mane to try to guide it. All the local ponies' manes were coarse and gave a good hold; but he longed one day just to ruffle his hands through the manes of those silver horses in the bishop's stables, which blew fine and silky in the wind. They would be of small help for holding onto and giving balance, but their manes were as beautiful as his little sister's long hair, and as silver as the sunlit glass in the cathedral or as some of the bishop's new English silver coin regularly brought into the town by the boatload and there loaded onto packhorses.

He had seen the new cathedral already rising and the old forcibly changed day by day, pulled down section by section, with extraordinary rapidity, so that quite quickly the safe cocoon of chapter buildings became open and unrecognisable. The old footings were literally excavated and re-formed to provide the foundations for the new.

He had always been taught by his parents to be wary of gossip and to avoid both it and the gossips, so already it was becoming second nature – except when he wanted to pick up news or rumours himself. But just as the cathedral buildings were changing daily, even faster flew the rumours about the town. And recently, the talk in the town had become beyond all imagining: battles and crown-wearings accompanied by killings and fires more incredible than those in the Old Testament from which his father told his children stories.

Brought up by his gentle parents to suspect gossip, the boy felt he had to ascertain some real truths, particularly whether it was real that the still quite young Bayeux bishop was helping his senior half-brother, the duke, to rule the kingdom of England. And only within the walls of the Church of Bayeux would he have the chance to learn the skills essential to achieving a position there. More, perhaps one day soon, he might manage to speak about these things to some servitor or stableman here who had indeed been in attendance on someone who knew: who perhaps had been himself on an expedition that wasn't simply the street talk of the boys or the over-hearings of the ale-wives. The clergy who knew, or at least those who knew most, always spoke together in private, after services, or before chapter. And although his father was one of these, he knew the canon could not be cajoled by anyone into divulging anything he was not intended to.

Thinking of his father encouraged him. With luck, he might see the canon in the distance sometime tomorrow, and he imagined a nod of approval from him. He must persist.

A little glimmer of bright starlight filtered through a small vent high in the eaves. He watched it, but it seemed fixed, not moving through the sky as his father had shown him some stars often did. If that star would stay and give him a point of light till he fell asleep, the eight-year-old felt he, too, could stay and see this through. Despite lacking physical comfort, stiff and straight as he had to be on his sacking of straw, yet drawing reassurance by the stable presence of the Northern Star, and tired out with all the new experiences of the day, the boy fell back asleep.

The senior boy was up first, rousing the rest of the dormitory, then turned back to Rannulf to make sure that he was stirring and starting to shake up the straw in the palliasse. But Samson was, in fact, no bully, and though he had a reputation throughout the school, it was not for that. Now in his early teens, Samson was far too conscious of the innate superiority of his own position in the school, his own studies, and the steady position his own father held in the cathedral hierarchy, to deign to descend to the role of a bully. Just tasked to make sure that this newcomer was well-drilled in the new routines quickly, so that he, Samson, could get on with the real business of life: convincing the canon schoolmaster that he was the brightest scholar the school had produced for years, as bright as his own elder brother, and that it was worth his father and the chapter's while to send him away to study in perhaps the greatest school of Europe, in the imperial city of Liege.

From there, there was nothing Samson could not then aspire to; his elder brother had recently been away gaining more knowledge and responsibilities in the great monastery of Bec from the Duke of Normandy's right-hand adviser, Master Lanfranc himself. Samson's family knowledge of this wider world meant his ambitions exceeded the little Rannulf's by far. The German emperor recruited his great churchmen from Liege and the greatest churchmen in the German empire might rise to rule a province and become a prince-bishop. Even that chance paled beside the real possibilities opening for those here in Bayeux now that their own Bishop Odo's half-brother, the Duke of Normandy, was crowned king in England. For Odo, created Earl of Kent, there was that whole region and indeed the whole country of England to administer according to William's will – if the coronation oath held good and the Duke of Normandy retained power long enough to get established.

But again, young Rannulf wondered. There had been a fire in the cathedral at the very time when the duke was crowned king. Rannulf remembered the many times in the Bible stories when God had expressed himself through fire. Was that not God's way of expressing disapproval?

The young bishop had introduced novel posts, customary elsewhere in the Roman Empire, to the chapter and diocese of Bayeux: offices to help him control the diocese, and Samson's father had been the man he had chosen to be Bayeux's first archdeacon as well as Treasurer. A strict, humourless man, fast aging, he was by no means an official the bishop liked to have close to him on feast days. Nevertheless, the bishop sought out his archdeacon's advice at most times; and the world knew, at least the Bayeux world knew, that Bishop Odo held him in high respect. He had given recent marks of high favour to the archdeacon's eldest son Thomas, whom he now made Treasurer, in preparation, it was thought, to try out the young man for greater things in England.

Samson's father had told him earlier that the young Rannulf was supposed to be an alert lad who had already received some teaching from his serious father and his gentle grandfather and who knew his letters and some simple Latin by word of mouth. Such minor feats by a small boy were, however, beneath the school star's notice. Samson was already fourteen and ready for the great world outside, and far too senior to be bothered with any rival, let alone such a young unschooled one (not to mention his own fervent resolution to live up to the strengths and foretaste of great deeds that were implicit in the name his father had given him).

"Hurry up there, young Rannulf. Get yourself washed now and ready to break fast, and be in school before prime. I want you there by the time the bell tolls. No talking to the other lads now," Samson ordered firmly, but with no malice.

Once in action and folded completely into the structure of the day, Rannulf had no time to feel despondent. In his queue with other boys for the cold water and for the bread – tasty and well-made of its kind but unlaced with any other goody – he became reassured and, as was usual with him, focused on at least keeping up with, preferably exceeding, his young contemporaries.

Now, some time on, it was Ascension Day. Special services were planned in the cathedral and the boys of the school were to attend at the back of the nave. In the days before this Thursday, the schoolmaster had attempted to explain its significance: when the cloud received Christ out of the disciples' sight, leaving them feeling isolated and bereft. Rannulf had not noticed Ascension Day before. He had always enjoyed the great processions of Whitsun, when the white flowers from the hedges and fields had briefly decked the town and the clergy themselves appeared robed in white and the whole world became a brighter prospect, heralding the summer. Now it seemed there was a lot to think about before that happened. Nevertheless, amidst the extra services, and the exalted concepts presented to him several times over the last two days, many of which, but not all, went over the head of the school's youngest boy, he still looked forward to the great feast of Whitsun. Far too busy in the days prior, the school was then due to have an extended holy day or holiday. Then he was due to go to his grandfather's some twelve miles out of town.

Visits to his grandfather made him feel manly. Often asked to help with the various tasks on his grandfather's land, he loved to vault on the small cobby horse that was his grandfather's jack of all work. As well as being his grandfather's mount, it did the harrowing of the cleric's portion of the village fields, and Rannulf was quite capable of riding the horse to its work and taking on the first hour or so of a task with little direction. As this Whitsun was late, if the weather held fine, the lad just might be able to help with some early haymaking as well. Being his first grandchild, his grandfather enjoyed talking to the boy as an equal; he sought to help him understand the way most people in the countryside won their living from the land, how they cultivated it, how to preserve the best seeds, which wood was best for fencing and which for repairing buildings and for making stools. He early helped him to recognise his letters, and without the boy even realising it, to make him, for some of the time at least, into a more considerate member of the family. More, Rannulf and his grandfather found themselves able to laugh together. In the evenings, they sometimes permitted themselves to laugh at the antics of the simpler villagers or of their children, telling the stories of the day to his grandmother. But more often, Rannulf's grandfather, the villagers' priest, and like them dependent on his forty acres or so of land, was exchanging his ready wit with the villagers in the fields and enjoying the situation alongside them, or giving smiling and supportive words to women with small children in tow and together with them savouring their children's antics.

This Whitsuntide, however, began in a way Rannulf had neither expected nor hoped for. First, his mother greeted him with a long, heartfelt hug accompanied with "Oh, Rannulf!" After a moment she went rapidly on, "I must tell you. You know how much I like to go with you to your father's parents and to get out of town, but I'm too tired and too busy at the moment. You'll have to go most of the way by yourself this time – I'm sure you'll manage as you've managed so well at school," came out quickly and as an unpleasant surprise to the boy, as his mother enjoyed the countryside and the opportunity to ride the pony almost as much as he did.

'Father will take you out of town to the first village and then he will arrange for you to go onward with someone from the bishop's stables. He said to me: 'Probably Bran: he's a lad they trust.' Then your grandfather might be able to meet you at St John's. You may have to walk on your own a little way in between, if the bishop's man is needed back at the stables. But it will be a great adventure.

'And you'll enjoy it', she added, as she saw her son's face fall. For a few moments Rannulf felt much less grown-up than he had anticipated feeling when he came back home. He couldn't help waves of disappointment, of almost rejection. He had loved the day's journey there with his mother in the past two years when, for once, he had her to himself. They had had such fun together – he trying to remember the names of the wild flowers which meant so much to her, then, when at a loss, him trying to think of better or funnier names for them, and her capping them – a game they had evolved naturally together and was peculiarly theirs.

To hide his chagrin, he rushed through the house to the small walled yard and garden to see whether that had changed much, and stood sniffing, taking in the lax growth of the herbs since he had last noticed them. The familiar background noises and smells helped him to regain some of his customary confidence. It then came to him that a ride alongside one of the bishop's stable men might be fun after all. The journey might be just the contact to enable him to visit the bishop's stables and learn more about those unique silver horses the bishop rode and the great ventures he had undertaken on them in England. He dwelt on these extraordinary horses for a few minutes; then told himself that, meanwhile, he must make sure that at home this evening he stayed especially close to his mother, while he could.

His father took him to the eastern town gatehouse. There outside the walls one of the bishop's stable lads was waiting on a lightly built dark grey dappled horse, leading an animal of almost white colouring, its uneven coat and hollows above the eyes, in contrast to the sheen of the coat of the lad's horse.

"Your father told me you could ride a bit so I thought we'd both be more comfortable if I gave you your own mount and I wouldn't have you bouncing around the pillion behind me. Anyway, this young horse would not have been used to that.' The young groom sensed that the boy was not being sent away in disgrace, but with loving care and he knew that this member of the cathedral chapter had the reputation of a quiet, kindly scholar.

He, turning to the father, added, "And he'll be all right on this one; she won't do anything unexpected, or not asked for. She's a good old girl.'

His father bent down to Rannulf, kissed him on the forehead, put his arm around his shoulders with a pat, then swung him gently onto the hard wooden saddle. 'Rannulf, please remember to give the letter to your grandfather first. May God go with you, and remain with you both.' And he gave the sign of the Cross.

Rannulf spent a little time getting used to the hardness of the saddle and the motion of the horse. The former was very uncomfortable; the little horse, however, would have been the smoothest ride he'd yet known but for the impediment of the saddle. Once he had adjusted himself to put the most padded part of his body onto the saddle, he found time to admire the groom's mount. It was obviously young and not used to the different sights and sounds of the busy road. Moreover, it was a young stallion and quite strong: when it was startled and shied, it moved quickly and powerfully but the groom rode it well and calmed most of its fears. It was evidently quite used to seeing wagon loads of hay coming in to the bishop's stables, but not at all used to the event of a part-load slipping off a wagon, causing great shouts of consternation from the waggoner and other road users.

'Is this mare quite old?' asked Rannulf some while after the stallion had recovered from the hay incident. 'And how old is your stallion'. The stable lad, relieved by these sensible questions and with respectful interest in his knowledge, answered readily enough. This small journey was proving a much easier task than his normal stable duties near the bottom of the hierarchy.

'I don't know quite how old; I think she's at least fourteen yet, which is a good age; with that coat she may be even older. They cling onto their winter coat a long time in spring if they are getting on. I suppose, like old people, they feel the cold. She's so sensible, and made herself so useful, and kept out of trouble. She's lasted a deal longer than most.'

After a few moments, he went on, 'My stallion is just a couple of years old or so. If all goes well, if he behaves well, and if I am seen to have trained him well, he will go to the bishop or one of his close companions, and I will have done myself some good in the stables.' He added rather proudly and, thinking that this lad with his quiet father was a safe enough confidant, 'I could even be travelling with the bishop next time he goes to England.'

All this was just the type of conversation most satisfying for Rannulf – practical knowledge, yet with the added lure of exciting future prospects. He quite forgot the disappointment about his mother and rode onwards, exhilarated. When they were out of the environs of the town and the roads had become quieter, it was only the odd bird, itself frightened by the movement of the horses, flapping out of the bushes, which spooked the stallion. He asked some more questions.

'Why was this mare kept in the stables so long when most of the bishop's horses were stallions?'

Again, the lad seemed glad of the chance to show off his knowledge. 'Oh, most of the stallions do come from the bishop's stud, and all the good mares stay outside for breeding. Some good ones are exchanged with other landowners. Others are sold locally as working horses. It depends on their quality. Top horses can get top prices; but you can't keep breeding from the same stock, otherwise they all get closely related, and weaker. This little mare was kept for breeding, but she never got in foal. But she was so well behaved, they thought she might be useful for us in town as a general-purpose animal (and for being ridden by the nervous young knights, and recruits too) especially to help train the frisky young horses and provide a steady lead for them. The youngsters are always better with an old one around rather than all the young 'uns getting each other silly and frightened together. So, we kept her.'

The young stableman was finding the younger lad was listening intently, and so carried on confidently.

'If this grey lives long enough he'll probably grow white like the mare you are on. They usually do. I think the dapple looks very smart and so do most of the bishop's friends, evidently. They all want these. But half of them don't realise they've got to be looked after to get to the stage of being part white and part dappled. They like them like that because they show up best in a procession or on the battlefield, whether they're showing off or getting their own knights to rally around them.'

They were now in open country. Rannulf rather nervously asked if the horses were allowed to canter.

'If we go very steadily, we could perhaps. But the last thing I want this young horse to do is fall into a wild pace. I probably would not be able to stop him until next Sabbath day. And he could take great harm in the meantime.'

He added, 'See that fence of sticks and brushwood over there, we will trot to there, carefully and slowly. You staying a little bit behind me, and see how that goes.'

Rannulf did exactly as he was bidden, and both horses managed calmly.'

'Well done', said the lad. 'We might do that again in the right place.'

About half an hour later, they came out of the forest at a place where the hay had been cut, and a brushwood fence separated the good meadow from rough scrub where sheep grazed. There, the stable lad suggested they might do the same: trot and go into a slow and careful canter if all went well. It did, and Rannulf found himself grinning from ear to ear, even before the stable lad pulled back to a walk and turned round to give him a friendly look.

'Good,' he said. 'That will do for today. I don't want him to get overexcited each time he goes out. Just used to being out and about, and varying things. We'll walk most of the way now.'

The stable lad became even more companionable now he realised that Rannulf could manage a horse and obey his directions even better than his father had implied. 'You know, if you are set to become one of the bishop's clerks and do much travelling with him, you won't be given a stallion like this but you could do worse than ask for a mare like the one you're riding, only much younger. One like her that is well-bred but unable to breed and you'll get a horse of the same quality as the stallions. Perhaps a little smaller. But if you treat a mare right, she is more faithful than most horses; you just have to be a bit sensitive with her. But I think you could be. And you could enjoy having your own horse that you can rely on rather than being given one of the throw outs from the cohort of knights when they have been injured or frightened. And they're always far too careless with the young ones.'

His grandmother gave young Rannulf the loving welcome he had hoped for, and all the praise and prestige which he relished – for managing the journey mostly by himself, without the company of his mother. Standing overlooking the village, his grandparents' small house was closer to the church than the others but of the same materials, stone and thatch, though twice the length. His grandfather stood outside, leaving his wife in her own way to resume her affectionate relations with her eldest grandson, content that his grandson had safely navigated the journey from Bayeux. He now turned back to the problem that he could affect; the timing and plan for the hay harvest. He was careful to note the coming clouds, and was wondering if the village's plans had progressed for the cutting, drying, and carrying later that week.

Rannulf's grandfather held forty acres or so of glebe and, like the rest of the villagers with an arable plot, was deeply concerned that the small area of natural meadow should produce a successful hay crop for the winter. From the villagers' own arable crops, they were compelled to pay to the Church, in effect to him, one-tenth of this crop, and also of the livestock they produced. But, working alongside the villagers, the priest knew their hardships and felt embarrassed to do anything other than quietly forgive many a tithe. Although he had been brought up in circumstances far grander than they, he knew the value of the cooperation between them all. The locals often relied on that for their survival and he had the sense and lack of arrogance to understand that what respect he retained was largely the result of a little leadership and his own inbuilt sensitivity, as much or more than his religion.

Last year, arbitrary demands for the new cathedral building and the wars in England had pushed them all to the edge and some of the poorest beyond. Their new harvest had been arbitrarily seized by the bishop's men with their oxen to carry it off. Some oxen had not been returned at all; other animals were brought back in poor condition. Several of those that had come back were unfamiliar animals, and disputes, still unresolved, arose over who was to receive them as more animals were missing than returned. No appeal to any law lord or court could help as the demands had been made at the command of no lesser men than the Duke of Normandy and the Bishop of Bayeux themselves, and their will was gainsaid by no one.

Soon the harvest would be on them again. Yet the villagers were short of oxen power and the issues still festered. Moreover, the Duke or the Bishop may yet return again without notice. There were times when the priest was deeply ashamed of his upbringing and his relatives who were so avid to win extra lands and wealth alongside their Duke and their Bishop, and who colluded with the brothers' every ambition. Yet, for his very living in charge of this small church and the two neighbouring churches he relied on these same relatives, and particularly on his landed brother, who was a tenant of the bishop, and could be called upon to fight for him. Their ambitious uncles, moreover, rode alongside the duke.

Put in this position, the priest could not openly share his worries or his sympathies with the villagers. His wife apart, it was a lonely life. But his gentle clerical son in Bayeux and his wife were his occasional confidants. And his joy. And he remained amazed at how his son managed to maintain his living at the cathedral without entering into the political scramble and jealousies that inevitably accompanied the ambitious bishop. His son's gentle mien, his father began to realise, nevertheless concealed a careful as well as a scholarly brain, entirely without political ambition, and for that, the father gave heartfelt thanks to his Maker.

The youngest son of a landholder brought up in his household and destined for the church, the rural priest was now long estranged from his elder brother, who had inherited the estate. For red-letter days, religious feasts, and when witnesses to land grants were assembled with feasts and formality, he was not invited. On one or two occasions, the younger man had not been, had refused to be, totally subservient to the elder brother and behind him, the ducal power. He could not be relied on. In the past, he had raised objections about the new terms on which his brother's tenants had discovered they held their lands; they had changed without regard to recognised custom or customary rents, and he had declined to put his witness to the new rentals. As a result, he and his young had been quietly, without fuss, but firmly and finally, cut off from family resources apart from this small living.

So, unusual for his background, the priest had, if anything, more sympathy with the immediacy of the villagers' problems, which were often his own, than with the requirements of his duke and bishop who wished to invade another kingdom. He did, of course, see the necessity of compliance, but not subservience. Forced into the church by reason of his younger birth, he discovered that he was still there by temperament and inclination.

And he was now reassured that his son, too, was managing thus far to cope, albeit in his own individual, quiet manner. He prayed that his three small grandchildren – if all went well, soon to be increased again in number – might also assimilate this from their upbringing. His son's wife, fortunately, was a wise woman herself in a down-to-earth way that her husband could never be. Not merely a confidant for her husband, but as the daughter of a small merchant in the town, she was more practical than her husband. Indeed, the father admitted to himself that his son could not be more impractical: despite all his own efforts to show him how he thought the world really worked. Access to the opportunities opening up in the currently fast-expanding Norman world often demanded the ability to walk a political tightrope, not merely a strong constitution, and he recognised that it was his son's wife, rather than his son, who had the determination to give her young family the best possible start. And he thanked his Maker for that blessing.

On his return, it was not with content that Rannulf heard the news that Samson was shortly bound for Liege. Somehow it disturbed him quite unreasonably, and he now seethed: he was in such a state that he was moreover getting furious with himself for feeling that way, for he knew himself to be out of control – which again he disliked. He would take himself through a part of the town where he was likely to be little known and walk back down by the river until he felt calm again. It would not do to face his peers at the school like this, nor his parents and their young family. He knew that his mother and father, in their different ways, did nothing but the best they could for him and that they could never afford to send him to Liege.

He had only been a scholar in the school for two years now and he could never expect that any such venture would ever be suggested for him. His own father, whilst quite as learned, was not in the same league as the archdeacon; he had neither the incomes, the power, nor the contacts to permit Rannulf ever to think of such intellectual excitement as was rumoured to be had in Liege, where the cathedral school and the two monastic schools were grouping themselves together and teaching something men were starting to call 'universal knowledge'. Not simply Bible studies and the great writers who stood as the Fathers of the Church, but also mathematics, music and the study and collection of legal documents. It was a venture Rannulf now knew some of his privileged fellows in Bayeux might take, a platform where he felt young clerks of enterprise would be bound to be noticed, and from which they might well gain fast promotion. Not to mention the knowledge that they could there acquire, deservedly giving them that notice. Sometimes, however hard he worked at the school, he thought he would never be able to catch up, simply because of their respective circumstances of birth.

He wove his way through the narrow alleys, gloomily trying to avoid the garbage, even aiming the odd kick at a pile as thoughts of Liege reverberated. But the very smells helped him back to his practical senses, always close to the fore with Rannulf. Feeling better, he started to jump the worst of the fetid puddles and when he mistimed one, he managed to laugh at himself and then enjoy the challenge as he sped as fast as he could towards the river. The river, the Aure, did not flow directly to the sea; rather, it turned west above the town and headed towards Ligny, where it joined the Vire, which emptied to the sea. Rather, the sea-going ships handling goods, soldiers and horses to and from Bayeux docked at Port-en-Bessin, a coastal inlet a few kilometres north of Bayeux. Goods were transferred by wagon, and animals and people simply walked or marched with the lucky ones riding on horseback. Goods were then stored in warehouses typically by the river.

As he leant on the corner of the parapet of the busy bridge, quite well out of the way of all but the largest wagons, he watched the seemingly endless activity. His feelings settled and he told himself firmly that he would simply have to make himself known some other way. The way things worked in the countryside, he could learn much from his grandfather. Also, the way things worked in the town, he could learn from his mother's mother, a strict old woman who had nevertheless managed to keep her husband's business afloat, although she was long now a widow.

Rannulf was more than a little nervous of her: she did not tolerate boys' tricks or humour. He felt no bond of affection there but he did note a little softening towards his sister and some material support to her, but none to spare.

The groom at the bishop's stables, the men down at the quayside in Port-en-Bessin and those organising transfers at the town warehouses; such people knew how their worlds really worked. There were those in Bayeux who talked of revenues and power and even with respect for the legal scholarship of Lanfranc and the philosophy of some Italian thinkers, but they did not give the same respect to where those incomes came from. Nor the logistics and manpower needed to move the silver, gold, corn and oats needed for these bold military acquisitive expeditions they so easily conceived, nor all those revolts that they took revenge upon, burning crops and barns without discrimination. They were without a thought as to how these destitute and subjugated peoples might yield them rents or taxes in the years to come. For the moment, might was right. But both horses, and ships, got worn out easily and needed knowledge and care for the speedy work they were commanded to do. Both currently got short shrift.

Thinking about such practical things, gaining real knowledge was only possessed by the boatmen, the waggoners and stablemen themselves. Perhaps Bran, who had accompanied him to his grandfather's place, might enable him to understand practical matters which his school-fellows, raised as Archdeacon's sons often were, might never need to concern themselves with; and might never well learn.

Sometime later, he reflected on the trust which had been given to him by Bran and his workmates down at the stables. He had taken good care of the eccentric old mare, which, although she refused to breed, had nevertheless, after a week or two, taken to him and his care and become much more manageable and, therefore, useful. So, when he approached Bran again about learning with the young stallions and especially how to train them into obedience, his skills had advanced almost unrecognisably, and Bran felt he could raise the topic again with his superiors. And so, Rannulf was given more trust and responsibility to handle one or two of the young horses. He succeeded in keeping most of these activities with the young horses shielded from the knowledge of his father, whose interests very much lay elsewhere. His mother was far too absorbed by her growing family and the last thing Rannulf wanted was to worry her in an area where she had no influence or powers, and neither did he! But his father did note his slow progress with his ability in Latin, whether it was the formal words of brief writs or the lack of ability with any of the monastic fragments of history that they had access to, not to mention the holy text itself. Although, in a way, it was the sacred texts, more rehearsed and memorised, that went into young Rannulf's mind.

At first, it was a matter of getting to know a couple of the young horses recently brought in from the field, ones that were neither known for aggression nor obedience, and to get them on Rannulf's side before they grew up too much and became proud of their own talents, and too assertive. It became months, even years, before Rannulf was fully trusted with most of the stallions. Even then, there were a couple, of course, the most beautiful as well as the more obstreperous, that everyone from Bran to Odo fixed their eyes upon. So, it was all the more difficult to progress those and to resist the pressure from Odo to give them to him for his personal retinue too early. If Bran yielded to those pressures and these two horses were not then receptive to their superiors' command, it would look bad for Bran. But Rannulf eventually became entrusted with these horses, to see if he could progress with them. He succeeded with one. But after the other, with shod feet, pawed a front foot hard with no particular purpose which struck him painfully on one foot, laming him, and another occasion kicked him from behind without much reason, he decided that his success with the one stallion was sufficient to carry his reputation. The other he would leave to more expert hands, which he did after explaining to Bran. But he began to think that the stallion that resisted discipline was certainly not going to suit Lord Odo long-term in many situations. And the flashing and rolling of the eyes, which did not diminish, confirmed this impression. The other animal, however, quite quickly learned one or two games Rannulf played with the handful of oats and chaff, which gave the horse not just an understanding of jokes with his handler, but also made him listen for Rannulf's words and the occasions when they were used.

Meanwhile, his father had been asked to pay a visit to the monastic house on St Michael's Mount where Scolland was Abbot. He had been sought out to accompany the newly appointed Abbot Scolland to St Augustine's on the edge of Canterbury, Odo's English seat as Earl of Kent. Scolland had been selected to lead the project commissioned by Odo in the early 1070s to create an embroidery (but always referred to later as a Tapestry) to commemorate the Battle of Hastings, which Odo wanted to unveil in Bayeux at the opening of the new cathedral. Canterbury offered secrecy to the project but, more importantly, was the home of many renowned, skilled embroiders.

On his return, his father had little time to eulogise the house of St Augustine's. As elsewhere, it was being rebuilt, or at least rethought. Young Rannulf was very jealous of his father's company and his mission to England, but his father was denied the indulgence of taking him along too and Rannulf could but hope to listen to stories of the most ancient of houses on his return. But that was not to be. Instead, his father wanted to talk to him, a teenage conversation you might say.

'Rannulf, I need to talk to you about your conduct around the church and with your fellows.'

His father received a responsive nod from his son, who stood waiting by his father's chair ready to listen, but already anticipating a cautionary warning, even a severe reprove.

'I know you are by nature exuberant and lively, very unlike me, much more like your mother, perhaps my father too. But I do wish you would control and heed your actions and words a little when you are at school or helping with clerical tasks about the Church and cloister. I know it's an exciting time. Our world, Normandy especially, is changing faster than I would ever have thought possible, certainly faster than I can take. I wonder how my clerical colleagues in England manage, and I daily pray for them and their work. I have always thought it is better to make oneself useful, to keep one's head down and not to be noticed is much safer. These lords of ours are selfish, ruthless men; you don't even have to make one slip. You just have to annoy them once or encounter them when they are in bad humour, and their temper can be dire. Whatever their pious words, the peace of God does not rule in their hearts or minds for long. They are men of action who want other men to fear and obey them. They are not forgiving. And, I fear, I would have neither influence nor silver to rescue you.'

Rannulf thought for a moment or two and then spoke as seriously and as carefully as he could muster. Seldom did he hear his father talk for so long. He knew he should respond in kind, and carefully.

'Father, I thank you. I appreciate what you said, but you must know, you obviously do know, that I am not of your temperament. I cannot contain myself and my energies. I do hope to make myself useful and respected: not sure at all whether I can become as respected as you are. I know you are respected within the cathedral. And you are respected at home more than

I can say and you surely know that too. But that wider world calls me: I long to see England, from where all this silver and treasure comes. But I also long to see their churches, which our Duke is now setting on fire, or our bishops pulling down, in order to raise them to the way of building that we have in Normandy. But I am still of your upbringing. Father, I'm not at all sure that this is right. Perhaps some clerks, like me, who have to try to put their demands into practice, can intervene between the great men and their arbitrary wills and find solutions that are more practical and less wasteful. Your father, without causing grief, manages to do that in his own way; something that does not cause such huge taxes and arbitrary confiscations from the peasants; something that respects the English and their worship. How can it be right to claim to be the heir of King Edward the Confessor and yet pull down the churches where the Confessor's people and lords worshipped and were buried in? All of these bishops need clerics like me to serve them and carry out their wills while they are at the great councils. I'm not a scholar like you, Father, but I feel I could do some useful work and, I hope, avoid arbitrary censure, as well."

His father was about to respond, as though in disagreement. So Rannulf spoke again. Now was the time for complete openness and to tell his father what had been obvious to him for some time, but he knew would be most unpopular.

'Also, Father, I must say to you that the time may soon come for me perhaps to go to England with Odo. I will try to tell you exactly how things go here, but as soon as the bishop – or the archdeacon – raise their little finger, Father, I have to say 'yes' to almost whatever it is, if I feel I am ready or nearly ready. But I will always try to look after you and mother whenever I can, if I survive.' Then he faltered and turned away, unable to control either his voice or his feelings, reluctant to show his weakness. He stared hard at the crack in the stone floor and repeated, 'I will always try to look after you and mother, if I can …' Then he added, '… and the others, of course'.

His father, moved, stood but turned away. Then turned back to Rannulf without letting him see his face and put his hands round his son's shoulders and gave them a long gentle squeeze. His father, too, could only repeat his own words.

'But please take care. I know you are brave and enterprising; too much so. But please, please take care.'

At that, he felt that neither could go any further at this point. Yet he worried that his son, whilst a lively and practical thinker, did not consider deeply the consequences of his actions, or of those of other people, so he added, 'For my soul's sake, for God's sake, take care'.

Sensing he had now gone a step too far, the father left the small room and the little house and strode down to the bridge where there was always too much bustle for anyone not in business to be heeded. He reminded himself that, as a fit man in his prime, he must show some leadership to his young family and not simply show himself as a weak pleader.

However, his last words did resonate with Rannulf. He had never before heard his father take God's name in vain.

Since the invasion of England in 1066, Bayeux had become important as the Normandy base for Bishop Odo supplying knights, materials and horses. Rannulf's skill with the horses was recognised by Bran and the other stable lads and as demand for new horses increased, so Rannulf was asked to help out more. On one occasion he was asked to give special attention to a couple of young mares. The mares were absolutely necessary as mounts for those who were in charge of the youngsters, but for the moment they were quite as feisty as the stallions, and had only a short space of time to learn proper behaviour and respect for their new young masters, and also for the boats they were to be taken on with the other young stallions. Rannulf wondered whether he could quietly recruit enough support to allow him to train these mares in an unobtrusive way that might nevertheless be appreciated by others. Anyway, as his ancient grandmother would say, he would have a damn good try. (He was distinctly nervous of her, but less so here in the stables, where she could not pry, safe from her influence, and where he could still have some influence of his own in a quiet corner without any of his family noticing – at least for a short time.) He spotted the older palomino mare, which had consistently resisted discipline amongst the assistant horses; and decided to start there. The mare swung round aggressively when she felt the management from the boy, but with his quiet persistence she quickly gave her attention, and indeed her hopes of a titbit, to him.

Rannulf's quiet unobtrusive work in the stables continued until 1080 when, now around twenty years old, to his surprise and delight, he was selected by Bishop Odo to accompany him on an expedition to suppress a rebellion in Durham. Rannulf had gained much experience working within the bishopric, both as an administrator, as an intermediary, and as a cleric in minor orders on top of his work in the stables; he was ready.

Chapter 2

Life under William the Conqueror

Bishop Odo's mission got the whole of Bayeux in a flutter in 1080. Odo had been at William's side in the battles of 1066 and had been given significant powers in England, first as Earl of Kent, one of the most vital counties of England, and one of the keys to its access. Since then, he was no less than Regent whenever the Conqueror returned to his first love and care, Normandy. Now Odo was commissioned to put down yet another rebellion in the north of England, and he was raising supplies and some troops in Bayeux to be reinforced by others in England to go into action as soon as possible. Three of his bishopric's clerks were to accompany him.

Of the two most senior, one was Rannulf. He had often accompanied Odo or represented him on diocesan matters of practical supply and jurisdiction in Normandy itself, most particularly to Caen and Rouen. There, he had worked with and experienced the practices of the senior ducal clerks. But this was to be another type of expedition altogether. He could not help being thrilled at the prospect of seeing and working in England itself. The element of danger, at his age, simply gave the expedition an aura of excitement.

But, Rannulf had not been selected 'from above', rather, the opposite! He had gone home one evening feeling disconsolate. His father had heard him complaining to his mother about his treatment at home, so he kept a good look out for minor posts in Normandy. However, he had sensed his son's desire to be part of the England adventure and had written to Odo with great purpose and, at last, had received a response. Rannulf had been specified for the role of Odo's secretary in England and to be as quiet as he could be about it. It was made quite clear that any grumbling at all would be remembered. Rannulf had explained his antipathy to a military campaign for himself and tried to keep a distance between himself and Odo's troops, but he was now required by Odo to be at his beck and call for things financial, and quite likely for other roles not yet explained. Rannulf remained unaware of his father's intervention. He knew he had no choice but to seize the opportunity.

That evening, Rannulf asked to speak to his father whom he knew would be better informed.

"I hope you are pleased with the assignment you have been given with Odo. But something is troubling you. What is it?" his father asked.

"I need to understand why this expedition has been ordered. My friends in the stables tell me a large rebellion in Durham was suppressed a few years ago. So, why again?"

His father paused, gathering his thoughts before replying, "Durham is the most important northerly town in England and part of the ancient Anglo-Saxon Kingdom of Northumbria. Northumbria is different from the rest of England. The ancient monastery of Lindisfarne, a part of Northumbria, was home of the much-revered St Cuthbert. It was the first place to feel the wrath of the warlike Viking invaders from across the seas. So, as time went on and all England faced these same invasion threats, Northumbria, reluctantly, agreed to accept the rule of a king of all England but on the condition they would retain much of their independence.

"It is a remote area, far from Winchester and London and Canterbury. However, Duke William knew from the outset that he needed their support in order to keep the Scots under King Malcolm from invading from the north and west. Given the influence of Viking settlers here in Normandy, you can imagine the Earl of Northumberland was wary of accepting Norman rule. Their uneasy truce fell apart in 1069 and the Northumbrians, under the Earl of Bamburgh, rebelled. There was much bloodshed on both sides. Eventually, a new leadership was established in that kingdom and Abbott Walcher of Liege was appointed Bishop of Durham. His diocese extended to all Northumbria. He had good connections with the local leaders; the chief among them even built a residence for the new bishop within the confines of the castle. He also succeeded in gaining the Earldom of all Northumbria, and was England's first Prince Bishop. But he proved to be a poor secular leader.

"When the Scots invaded Northumbria again last year, they met with no opposition and plundered the land. The local leaders turned on Walcher. In an attempt to mend fences, Walcher met with these leaders at a place north of Durham. But it was a bad-tempered meeting – important people were killed on both sides, including Walcher. The local population rose in support of their leaders and have been intent on destroying everything Norman; people and property. That is why Odo has been ordered to quickly assemble a large force to go to Durham to restore William's authority."

"But surely that will not be enough to restore peace?" Rannulf replied.

"You are right," said his father. "Our Duke has also ordered his eldest son, Robert, to lead another force to ensure that the Scots have fully retreated. He will also begin the construction of a new castle at the crossing point over the River Tyne to the north of Durham. And he will seek a meeting with King Malcolm in an attempt to secure a more lasting peace. But these are military solutions. A lasting peace will need a different approach." Given the two had never spoken of such matters before, the father asked, "Has that helped, my son?"

"Yes, father. But what do you think will happen in Durham, in Northumbria, after this expedition?"

His father paused, wondering whether to share some of the talk he had heard even that day with his colleagues in Chapter. He said, quietly, "It is said that our Bishop favours the appointment of William St Calais, now an Abbot of the Abbey in Le Mans, as the new Bishop of Durham. Both Odo and Duke William know him well as he was born in Bayeux and studied first at the very school you attended. It is early days. St Calais is a respected administrator, much stronger and worldly-wise than Walcher; perhaps a diplomat. But I doubt if Duke William will want to appoint him Prince Bishop, at least not yet.

"Beyond that, I do not know. I am pleased you have been given this appointment. But be careful. There will be much violence and killing for sure. You will need to avoid being sucked in. Use your skills to discover what the local people are most worried about and find a way to tell Odo. He may be fearsome, but I think he will listen."

The following morning, Rannulf was thrilled to learn that he would be allowed to take the palomino mare as his mount. Earlier, she had been gathered in with the others to carry some weight as a more mature animal, but she felt both imprisoned and ignored and did not behave well. But she had responded to his touch, and now she was his! He did not relish the long sea journey – his first – but he survived.

Once in Durham, Rannulf immediately felt moved by the wild beauty of the peninsular and its surroundings. But to Rannulf's dismay, destruction and death were inevitable. The old minster, close to the bishop's residence, was damaged; other buildings were destroyed, people injured, killed and some imprisoned. Odo occupied the bishop's home within the castle compound and his troops occupied other outbuildings and the open high ground around the castle and the old church.

All Rannulf could do was to help make the process as speedy and acceptable as he could without getting involved in or supporting the fighting; he preferred talk, compromise, and mediation. In this, he was quite successful.

Escape from the acrid smoky air into the fresh mountain blast proved a brief but lively escape for him. He clung to the readiness to take a message from the distressed peasantry and ride almost unaccompanied across the moors, his stable boy on hand to take a message to Odo if required. Everyone wanted just one thing: protection: protection from the Scots and protection from the Norman soldiers. The message back to Odo was the same each time.

Rannulf certainly looked with knowledge at the breeding mares, here mostly of the chunky sort, turned out by the canons for the winter. He would have liked to get involved in developing the potential of the young stock, much as he had done in Bayeux. He certainly wanted to avoid being given any responsibility for the adult horses, which would undoubtedly create the risk of getting him drawn into military action. But he had no time for any of that.

Feeling low, he thought out where he could find rest and consolation and some little independence from the contemporaries who surrounded him; he did manage to find a small bolt hole: the old but undamaged stables used by the canons. Just as in Bayeux, he simply weaved his way in with the hay and straw and found respite.

In these quiet moments, he could speculate about how he would go about rebuilding, what type of fruits might survive in this climate, and many other things. He was now completely sure that he could not tolerate any form of fighting. Much needed to be done. Above all, he wanted to improve the lives of the local population, which he wished he could someday be part of.

Whilst in Durham, William St Calais was nominated later that year as Bishop of Durham and his consecration was completed by the start of 1081. Rannulf was delighted, believing that St Calais' reputation as a skilled administrator and diplomat would help build trust with the local people. But as his father had anticipated, St Calais was not appointed Prince Bishop.

Odo had also told Rannulf that he should give service to Queen Matilda whose own force, which was permanently assigned to her, had also been called on to assist in the Durham mission. Serving two masters was quite a stretch but he succeeded, and when Odo finally returned to Bayeux in 1081, Rannulf went directly to Winchester.

It was the last time he met Odo for, back in Bayeux, Odo's ambitious and adventurous nature got him involved in leading a curious expedition on his own account to Italy, rumoured to concern the Papacy. Whatever the reason, his stepbrother, the King, took a dim view of it; he imprisoned him in Normandy and stripped him of his lands in England.

Although his service to Odo was at an end, his work for Matilda was obviously appreciated. Indeed, the record survives of one of Queen Matilda's charters which mentions him particularly and favourably. He was told to go to Winchester, where the Queen had arranged for him to meet Walkenin, the Bishop of Winchester, a relative of the King.

No doubt influenced by the Queen's favourable report, Rannulf was ordained Deacon, the first rung on the major order in the Roman Catholic Church. He dared to dream. William St Calais was only a member of the deaconate when he was appointed Bishop of Durham. Rannulf was given administrative charge of the old Minster, St Swithins, following the appointment of Simeon, the Prior, brother of Walkenin, as Abbot of Ely in

1082. The Bishop had already commissioned the construction of a new minster, which would become his cathedral when completed.

Rannulf's energy and ability to manage multiple tasks were noticed. He did not mind being asked to struggle with something difficult. At the moment, he did feel that the tasks allotted him were a battle but also that if he did manage to clear one or two commissions it would be noticed and commended. Soon, Maurice, the King's Chancellor, head of the Chancery and responsible for the drafting and writing of all the King's letters, charters and writs, became aware of Rannulf's skills and appointed him as a clerk. He was able now to develop his writing skills, improve his working knowledge of Latin and, above all, to rapidly build up his understanding of the legal system.

His work chiefly concerned land and related financial issues. He developed a deep understanding of the feudal system and the role of the Sheriff as the King's representative in the shires in charge of the Shire Courts and the lower Hundred Courts.

Rannulf proved to be a loyal, trusted and effective clerk, the rising star amongst the Chancery royal clerks. Maurice's regard for him was manifested in a special, unusual, assignment which he was given a few months before the King's council meeting to be held in Gloucester in December of that year, 1085. The King had asked Maurice to conduct a survey of his lands attached to the church of St Martin le Grand in Dover. If it could be done well, his hope was that the same approach could be repeated with other surveys. He wanted it to be thorough with enough detail to help determine the value of the land and how that could be improved. But the King also wanted to know how these facts and assessments had changed since the time of his cousin, Edward the Confessor, and from the early days of his Conquest after he had re-assigned the land in the kingdom to his loyal supporters to the present day. He needed the brightest and best clerk who would combine thoroughness, with haste and secrecy.

Maurice selected Rannulf.

Maurice instructed him to examine not only the papers held in the Treasury here in Winchester, in Dover, but also in the Shire court under the Sheriff of Kent and the Hundred courts that held jurisdiction over Dover. Rannulf realised that Dover was important, special to the King. His army had destroyed much of the old church and the town as his soldiers spread out from Hastings in 1066. William realised the potential of Dover as an important port and St Martins held the greatest part of the land in and around the town. He decreed that he, and he alone, would have the authority to appoint the Abbot. He would brook no interference from the Archbishop of Canterbury or the Church of Rome. The church held huge influence in the town and he wanted to harness that. But Rannulf was smart enough to realise this could not be the sole or perhaps even the main reason for this assignment. The King's interest in land value suggested a different reason; perhaps how to increase taxes from the land. Rannulf set off on his trusted palomino mare accompanied by one of the scribes from the Chancery scriptorium. Maurice seemed pleased with Rannulf's report and took Rannulf with him to present it to the King. The King seemed well pleased. Pleased enough to reward Rannulf with his appointment as Keeper of the King's Seal. It was the Chancellor's responsibility to approve the documents issued in the King's name by affixing the royal seal as a sign of its authenticity. Rannulf must guard it with his life. With this appointment, he would also oversee the work of the Chancery scriptorium and be the Chacellor's deputy. It was a huge step up for Rannulf.

In December 1085, by order of King William, the compilation of The Great Survey, later popularly known as 'Domesday', was commissioned. A task force within the Chancery in Winchester was quickly established. Bishop St Calais of Durham would be an important part of the project's leadership team; he was also a close adviser to the King and his regent when the King was not in the country.

When St Calais had first arrived in Durham he found the old Anglo Saxon minster in a poor state, and the canons in charge in the absence of a bishop lacked discipline and any sense of leadership. He decided that he should reorganise the church from a minster run by canons to be run as a monastic church. To achieve this, he would establish a new monastery, an Augustine monastery, to be formed by monks from the Augustine monasteries at nearby Jarrow and Wearside and reassign the canons to churches elsewhere in his diocese. Several of these canons later formed a collegiate church in a nearby estate of the bishop, Aukland.

Armed with the support of the Archbishops of York and Canterbury, he went to Rome to gain the Pope's approval. He issued a charter in 1083 establishing the new monastery, with its Prior to be elected independently by the monks and the monastery endowed with sufficient land from the bishop's own vast estate to enable it to flourish independently. The Prior would be in charge of running the cathedral, organising the church services and deputising for the bishop in his absence. Fortunately, by the time St Calais had been summoned to lead the Domesday project, his plans had been implemented and a prior elected. He had also begun to develop his ideas for a new much larger monastic church to be dedicated to St Cuthbert that would also become the final resting place of St Cuthbert and St Bede.

Having seen St Peter's whilst in Rome, he had set his sights on building what would be the largest church in England and that little bit longer than St Peters. It would be his seat as Bishop and would be known by the modern name of Cathedral rather than simply 'church'. But with St Calais' summons to lead this new task force, those plans were put on hold.

Maurice, who was elected Bishop of London at the same King's council meeting in Gloucester, told St Calais of Rannulf's work for the King at St Martins and the King's expectation that this should be the model of how to conduct the survey throughout the country. Not surprisingly, St Calais invited Rannulf to join the team. Rannulf was thrilled. Opportunity knocked. St Calais had assembled a strong team, which became a powerhouse in the realm. Samson, his bed fellow in his first days at school in Bayeux, as well as Rannulf, was also to be part of the large assembled team. The Survey's main objective was to record the annual value of every piece of landed property and the resources in land, labour force, and livestock from which the value was derived. The Survey also served to document the many changes in ownership that had taken place since the Conquest. Thus many historians consider Rannulf to be one of the leading candidates to have been the Mastermind of Domesday.

Much had changed in England since 1066. Perhaps the King was simply inquisitive to know what he now held. More likely he needed to know how to raise more revenue to fund his vastly expanded army as he built up his defences against the possibility of a Danish invasion. Perhaps he also needed to know exactly how he could feed these soldiers now spread widely throughout the country. The King decreed that the final written document would be the definitive record; unalterable. In time, its completion was associated with The Day of Judgement; finality. Hence the more popular name of Domesday!

The country would be divided into seven regions. Seven teams, each under the leadership of a Commissioner, were to be formed to conduct the survey, one for each region. The Commissioners were all senior and trusted allies of the king and were to be from an area well away from the one assigned to them to ensure impartiality. They were each given judicial powers from the Royal Court to hear evidence under oath in the Shire Courts. Bishop St Calais led the South West team, for example.

The King demanded that the survey be completed and presented to him within two years. In practice, this meant that the collection of all the information must be completed by the end of 1086 to allow time for the scribes to collate the data and write the report by the end of 1087. The sheriffs in each county in a region would be responsible for the collection of the information. Terms of reference were agreed in Winchester and sent to the sheriffs specifying exactly what information was needed, how it was to be collected and how it needed to be organised. The sheriffs already held information pre-dating the Conquest on the geld payments and on the land organisation down to the manor level; more detailed information would be available in the Hundred courts and from representatives of all the tenants in chief and their tenants who would be ordered to comply. All this information, once collated, would then be presented in writing and under oath to the Commissioners sitting in the Shire Courts of their region supported by their own small team of clerks and scribes.

It was in this phase that Rannulf shone. He did much of the analysis of the information to be presented, resolving issues ahead of hearings where he could and briefing the Commissioners on lines of enquiry to be examined in court. The Shire court hearings each lasted several days.

It was hard work, but overnight, the touring entourage was well entertained and fed.

Rannulf was bright and good-looking. Inevitably, he began to enjoy the company of women. Over time, he had several mistresses; his favourite was Avelva, also known as Aelgifu.

His colleagues gave him the nickname 'Flambard', a flame at work and play! He stood out amongst the other clerks for his intelligence and good looks, but more importantly his assertive and persuasive personality, which enabled him get things done well and quickly.

'Flambard' means torch bearer, incendiary or devouring flame. But the origins of his nickname vary depending on who is writing.

His colleagues would say it reflected his high-spirited personality, whilst some of his critics resented that Rannulf, of low birth, ordered the nobility around. Each to his own. 'Flambard' stuck!

Domesday included, of course, Rannulf's own land. Land and benefices were the normal payment for royal clerks. He held land primarily in Hampshire but also small parcels in Berkshire, Oxfordshire, Surrey, Wiltshire and Somerset. In total, it amounted to 25 hides, over 1000 acres. A slight bantering association between Samson and Rannulf is certainly evident in the Domesday Book, albeit not prominent. Samson was probably the person to persuade the Domesday scribe to slip into the record on Rannulf's property in Hampshire the words 'the tax which no one can evade', in the margin of that page. Some areas of the country were omitted from the scope of the Survey; London, Winchester and the 'wilder' areas of Durham and Northumberland were not included in Domesday. But, for example, a survey of Winchester was completed early in the 12th century; this written survey survives and shows how Samson had taken over Rannulf's 'former much enlarged tenement outside the north gate'.

To quote the Winchester survey: 'there was a street then in King Edward's day along which the burgesses used to lead their horses to water but the Bishop of Durham (Rannulf) incorporated that Street into his own tenement; but now the Bishop of Worcester (that is Samson) holds the tenement'.

By summer 1087, the first great book was completed but the second, to cover East Anglia, was not yet completed. This area, which included Norfolk, Suffolk and Essex, had proved complex and Rannulf had been assigned at the request of the aged and ailing Abbot Simeon of Ely to assist Simeon in the administration of the Abbey's vast estates and specifically to help him meet the demands and opportunities of the Domesday survey. The Abbey of Ely had experienced great difficulties following the Conquest. Its lands were spread out over six counties, including Norfolk, Suffolk, and Essex in the East Anglia region. The King's soldiers had taken many parts of the Abbey's lands for themselves; much effectively stolen. There followed in 1071 an uprising against the Normans centred on Ely, one of whose leaders was Hereward the Wake. The Abbey sided with the rebels. Much damage was done. William supported the appointment of his relative Simeon as Abbot in 1083, not as an act of confrontation but as an act of reconciliation. Simeon had his own ideas of how to achieve that. He initiated the building of a new church, later to become Ely Cathedral, to be funded entirely by the Abbey's own income. But he also set out to restore the lands stolen from the Abbey by the early Norman conquerors. The King's Survey presented an opportunity to put the Abbey's case for restitution forcefully to the Commissioners as they heard the many cases before them in each of the six counties. So Rannulf came to help. The reports on the Abbey's submission were later combined into a single report, a mini-Domesday some would say, called the Inquisition of Ely. It is a report still in existence today and the only report that documents the details of the data to be collected in the Survey.

But in late summer, King William died and all work on the Survey stopped to await orders from his successor. Though the second book would be completed later, what had been achieved was truly amazing.

Rannulf returned to the Chancery. William St Calais had already returned to Durham to begin work, with a newly appointed prior, Turgot, on making his dream for a new cathedral a reality.

Just as Rannulf's first expedition to England in 1080 proved a pivotal moment in his life, so King William's final deathbed wishes in 1087 were to define Rannulf's future in ways he could not then imagine. William had been on a military foray in northern France when his horse reared forcing him to land awkwardly as he fell back into his saddle. William had become obese and as he landed on his saddle, his stomach and vital organs were squashed badly against its hard, tall, wooden pommel. He suffered serious internal injury, the severity of which was not understood by his companions. He fell ill and returned to Rouen. His health deteriorated. A few weeks later he died.

As he lay dying, he made some surprising decisions. Firstly, at the behest of his other step-brothers, he pardoned Bishop Odo, who was imprisoned in Bayeux. Secondly, as expected, he appointed his troublesome older son, Robert, as heir to the Duchy of Normandy, the traditional lands of his family, but surprisingly he did not appoint Robert as heir to his whole kingdom, deciding to appoint his middle son, William Rufus, as heir to the Kingdom of England. Rufus left for England immediately to secure his new role.

After the King's death, everyone at his bedside fled, stealing everything in the room in the process of returning to their respective home bases to plot the protection of their wealth and position in the light of the new order. It was a typical medieval case of 'The King is dead, long live the King'. Only the future mattered. It was sometime later that a passing knight found William's naked body and made arrangements for it to be embalmed.

William's younger son, Henry, was left no land, though he was left coin. He was the only son to attend the funeral held in Caen. In truth, it was the ecclesiastics, whom William had long supported, who dominated the presence at the burial service. History records it as a comedy of errors, but to those present it was shocking.

The service was brought to a dramatic halt by a member of the congregation who insisted on being heard. William lay in a part of the Abbey that had once, before the rebuild, belonged to the objector, a well-recognised follower of William. The Caen authorities now agreed that the land had been improperly taken from him and that the King's body lying there was totally wrong. The wrong was righted. The service continued. But worse was to come.

By tradition, the King's body, by now already putrefying and sadly smelly, was lying on an open bier ready for burial in the below-ground crypt. But the bloated body was now too big to fit into the pre-prepared stone sarcophagus. As it was forced in, the nauseous gases inside were forced out. The burial was hastily completed.

Chapter 3

England under William Rufus

William Rufus moved quickly to claim his inheritance as King of England. After occupying the Treasury in Winchester, he moved to Westminster to plan his coronation; he was crowned King William II in Westminster Abbey just two weeks after his father's death. Although Rannulf had expected, like many others, that Robert would be the appointed heir to both England and Normandy, he respected the Conqueror's decision and was ready to serve the new king, Rufus. He had worked hard on Domesday and was keen to remain in the Chancery ready to help Rufus take it to the next stage. Rufus was well aware of his skills and immediately appointed him Keeper of the King's Seal once more. But Rufus' immediate priority was responding to the evident unease caused by his father's dying wish to split the governance of his kingdom.

Many of his tenants in chief, the landed barons, held property in both England and Normandy and were now faced with the prospect of split loyalties in what was well-known to be a fractious relationship between Rufus and his elder brother Robert. They preferred a unified kingdom and tended to favour Robert's claim. Odo, now free, and with much of his land restored to him by Rufus, held similar views and also returned to England. But Odo was intent on sounding out opinions amongst the English barons for a challenge by Robert.

Eventually, Odo emerged to lead a rebellion on Robert's behalf. He raised a force in England and Robert a force in Normandy. Robert sold a part of his duchy in Normandy to his brother Henry to raise funds for the military venture. Their plan was for Robert's force to sail to England landing at Pevensey then march to Odo's headquarters at his Rochester Castle to join up before confronting Rufus' forces. But bad weather in the summer of 1088 prevented Robert's fleet from setting sail. Rufus seized the opportunity to besiege Odo's castle forcing him to surrender before reinforcements could arrive.

The drawing shows Odo leading his soldiers out of the castle after his surrender. Robert had lost and lost badly; he wasn't even there. Rufus was wise in victory, permitting Robert to retain his inheritance in Normandy and be free to return to England as he wished, in return for swearing his loyalty to Rufus as King of England. Odo was banished to Normandy for good, losing his estates and influence in England.

One problem remained for Rufus. Initially, all the English bishops had sided with him in confronting Robert's forces. But unexpectedly, the Bishop of Durham, William St Calais, withdrew his support and returned with his knights and soldiers to Durham. Unlike Bishop Odo, St Calais was no warrior, but he was obliged, as a tenant-in-chief to the king, along with other senior churchmen and the barons, to provide services to the king in return for being granted their large estates. Typically, these services included what was known as a knights' fee; the obligation to provide a defined number of trained, equipped knights and their support foot soldiers when demanded by the king. Rufus thus saw St Calais' withdrawal as an act of treason and held him to account.

Meanwhile, Rannulf had not been idle. In early 1088, he was assigned to supervise the large estates of the New Minster at Winchester after the death of its Abbot. Later that year, he took on the administration of the estates of Ramsey, all alongside his continuing to help Abbot Simeon at nearby Ely. Rannulf's ability to administer several great estates simultaneously was noted, not least by the new King. Rufus now turned his attention to his finances. It was probably then that the idea emerged for Rufus to delay filling any bishop vacancy, thereby enabling revenue surpluses to be sent to the Treasury to build up the funds for the defence of his realm and pay for his ambitions in northern France. Like his father, William the Conqueror, Rufus had continued to levy the Danegeld, which had evolved into a form of land tax under the Saxons after the threat of invasion by the Danish Vikings had all but disappeared. But the Danegeld was not sufficient. Rufus was loath to increase this unpopular tax but this new idea, though not new in other parts of Europe, would target the wealthiest, most notably the church, and might fill the financial gap.

In 1089, Archbishop Lanfranc of Canterbury died. Rufus decided to hold the position vacant and sent Rannulf there to appropriate the revenues of the Canterbury estate. On his first trip to Canterbury, Rannulf remembered his father's affection for this place. He liked the idea of his father coming home to that community if it could be managed; and, of course, Rannulf, 'Flambard', to obtain satisfaction for his father, managed it.

Bishop Odo of Bayeux had strong ties with St Augustine's, and this house was meant to be civilised and gentlemanly. Many of the tenants of St Augustine were contacts of Odo when he was in Kent, either of a military or land-holding connection with Odo. Rannulf would find it easier to check on his father's lifestyle and contentment at St Augustine's than in most places.

Shortly after this visit, Rannulf returned to his home in Bayeux to tell his father what he had arranged. To his delight, both his parents were pleased. In contrast to his father's studious and retiring nature, his mother, the daughter of a still active baker widow who liked her shop more than her grandchildren, was lively, and anxious to see as much of the world as she was able though happy to stay in Bayeux. Whilst there, he made contact with a girl he had seen on an earlier visit. Ever since he had first come across the girl, who was an acquaintance of his sister's, physically very like her, cavalier in action, with fair hair but willing to listen to him on important occasions, he was attracted to her. Rannulf resolved to marry her, but first, he needed to check protocol with the bishop or the senior members of the chapter.

The Pope in Rome had decreed that all members of the major orders of the church should remain single, but his church in Bayeux had continued with the old practice. Odo was married, and so was his father and many others there. They approved of his plan. The girl's name was Celestine or Celest. Within two years she had borne him two sons, Thomas and Elias.

Relations between the three royal brothers, Robert, William and Henry, fluctuated constantly depending on their respective ambitions towards each other. Land in Normandy and northern France was always at the centre of any shift. Rufus was clearly angry at Robert's failed attempt in 1088 to seize his English crown and exacted revenge three years later, invading Normandy with a force sufficiently large to force Robert to the negotiating table. They negotiated the Treaty of Rouen in which William was awarded land and castles in Normandy and William agreed to help Robert regain lands in neighbouring Maine.

The Treaty also tried to resolve practical issues affecting the barons where they held estates in both kingdoms. Finally, both nominated each other as heirs to their respective kingdom thus raising the prospect of a united kingdom. Yet again Henry was excluded from any of the discussion. Not surprisingly, Henry retaliated and war broke out in 1092 between Henry and his two brothers. But the apparent reconciliation between William and Robert quickly evaporated. Indeed, William and Henry grew closer as Robert began to turn his attention to planning a crusade to the Holy Land.

Around this same time, Rannulf was appointed Dean of a new priory to be built at Twynham, also known, even then, as Christchurch. Twynham was an important port with a safe harbour and was at the confluence of the Rivers Avon and Stour. The priory was home to twenty-four canons. Rannulf decided that as canons died, they would not be replaced and the money saved would help fund a new priory. He wanted the new priory to replace several older churches in the area, which would again illustrate Rannulf's eye for cost savings and that the new priory was not simply an imposition of Norman church design replacing Anglo-Saxon, the practice of

The 900th anniversary of the Priory Church was commemorated in 1994 with the unveiling of a sculpture now to be seen in the Priory Gardens. The sculpture is shown in this photo; one of the four sides shows Rannulf ringing a bell whilst looking down on a newly married couple.

which, in his youth, he had been critical. A significant step in his ecclesiastical career, it gave him early hope that he could one day rise to the level of bishop, perhaps even replace St Calais in Durham, a place now close to his heart.

A while later, a sign of his growing value to Rufus, Rannulf was appointed head of the college of secular canons of St Martin le Grand in Dover, a place he had visited and surveyed in 1085. To hold such positions at the two most important ports on the south coast signalled his quiet rise in the English church.

In 1093, Rufus suffered a serious illness. He feared that his delay in appointing a successor to Lanfranc had cursed him, so to give thanks for his recovery he appointed Anselm, brilliant but a strong supporter of the new Pope's policies, to be the new Archbishop of Canterbury. It was a move Rufus lived to regret; they were forever at odds not least because Anselm was a fervent supporter of the new Pope's goal of eliminating the huge influence European kings had in church affairs, not least a king's presumed right to nominate a new bishop.

Anselm also wanted to establish the supremacy of Canterbury over all the bishops in England including York and Durham. He also supported the Pope's call for members of the priesthood to be celibate. Acceding to Anselm's demands would also scupper a key plank of Rufus' money-raising schemes. It put Rannulf on a collision course with Anselm, too, and he was soon issuing writs in the King's name against Anselm, one even being on the day of his enthronement. Not surprisingly, Anselm disliked Rannulf. He labelled him 'almost illiterate', but this was probably just a cheap jibe at Rannulf's lack of the elite's classical education in Latin and the Arts. History records that, later, Anselm told the Pope that the nickname Flambard came from Rannulf's cruelty, which Anselm likened to a consuming flame. One presumes that Anselm's use of the word 'cruelty' referred to Rannulf's role as the ruthless frontman for Rufus' financial ploys targeted at the bishoprics and monasteries. There was no evidence that would suggest Anselm was referring to physical cruelty but Anselm had used his skill with words to good effect.

Rufus realised that he needed to strengthen his hold on Durham, a town crucial in countering threats to his Kingdom from both the feisty folk of Northumbria and the Scots. He also recognised the skills of St Calais, a much stronger and more capable leader than Walcher. So, also in 1093, Rufus reinstated the exiled William St Calais as Bishop of Durham and elevated him to the role of Prince Bishop.

Although his diocese still extended to all Northumbria from the Tees to the Tweed (which formed the border with Scotland), Rufus had decided that in civil powers, Northumbria should be divided. The area north of the Tyne would become known as Northumberland with its own earldom. The area to the south between the Tees and the Tyne together with some other lands within the new Northumberland, previously held by the Patrimony of St Cuthbert, notably Northamshire and adjoining Islandshire (which included Lindisfarne), would become known as the Palatinate of Durham. St Calais, as Prince Bishop had temporal rights in the Palatinate usually exclusive to the monarch. Most important, these lands would not be subject to the king's geld.

St Calais immediately set about implementing his plans for the new cathedral. In August 1093, he and Prior Turgot laid the foundation stone. St Calais also agreed on a new plan with Turgot whereby he, the bishop, would take responsibility for raising the cash for the cathedral and its construction, whilst Turgot, on behalf of the monastery, would finance the building of the new monastery buildings adjoining the cathedral. In return, St Calais assigned new lands and rights to the monastery to enable them to take on their part of the project. For unknown reasons, this commitment was never documented. And, in recognition of

Turgot's help, Turgot was appointed Archdeacon of Durham giving him the bishop's delegated powers for administering all the churches in the Durham area.

Also in 1093, Simeon, the Abbot of the Benedictine Abbey in Ely and brother of the Bishop of Winchester, died aged 93. When Simeon had first been appointed there, the area was still a hotbed of resentment from the Norman ravaging of their lands where Hereward the Wake had seven years earlier led fierce resistance. Simeon had sought to rebuild relations and, in 1090, commissioned the re-building of the Abbey church along the same lines as that at Winchester. Rannulf, of course, knew the Abbey's estates and finances well, but now he was put in charge whilst Rufus once again delayed appointing a successor. But this was not well received. Without their Abbot to lead them, and perhaps unsure of Rannulf's instructions, the monks decided to halt construction of the new church. Work eventually restarted in 1100 when a new Abbot was appointed after Rufus' death.

Seeing less and less of Rannulf, his young wife, two sons and his mother had decided to join him in England, in Ely. As Normans, they would all be at risk in Ely, and he needed to get safe accommodation for them. Typical of many a young man, he suddenly realised how isolated they were in Ely and decided that their home, however temporary, should be in Winchester, which was central to wherever his growing list of assignments took him.

For now, they must take some safe lodgings just outside the centre of the city, and wait there calmly till he could get further information to them. He told his mother, who would liaise with them when she could, that it might well be a matter of a few weeks rather than hours before there was a plan. Once they were in Winchester, he needed to return quietly to Ely.

His ambition to be Bishop was growing, but privately. He hoped that his early command of the abbey estate of Ely might give him the possibility of eventually placing these two young sons into a known position in the church. His mother had accompanied the two children, to support them in every practical way. He was glad of her presence. She had appeared briefly in the background and now awaited instructions and further orders from her lord. He had been shaken to see her appear a day or two back, but now he was very glad to see her in the flesh and be reassured, even more so by the two small boys, who were starting to mean something to him. When he had established exactly where their longer-term lodgings were to be, he folded both boys and then his wife in their customary long slow hug.

He made Celestine aware that he had now received some hints of nomination for high office, but in these circumstances, everything was tenuous. He was earnestly hoping that he might one day earn a bishopric, so where better to be than Winchester.

Celest seemed to be aware of the importance of his aim; how he did not know. He was so proud of his young fair-haired partner; he also wanted to care for her because she had not yet become an integral part of the ecclesiastical structure. He had taken on responsibility for the girl's happiness, but there still were other layers of responsibility in several directions. Celestine, however, could not settle; she also saw little of her husband as his duties took him away most of the time. Soon, they returned to Bayeux.

Rannulf's importance to Rufus had grown rapidly, not just because of his efficiency, but because Rufus trusted him – trusted him not to siphon of revenues for his own gain, which many of the other royal clerks did. They also enjoyed each other's company. They had a shared sense of humour and energy for life. So, it was in 1094, as Rufus prepared to renew his military actions in Normandy, that he had uniquely been tasked with raising money from the fyrd: the pool of reservists the King could call on for military service to him. Each parish had to fulfill its obligation on demand of the King.

When called up, each parish had to give each man ten pounds to pay for his food and keep. But when the forces were assembled near Hastings, Rannulf's scheme was to collect all the ten pounds from each man and return the men to their homes, instead enabling the King to spend the money on hiring mercenaries at lower cost in France. The accord between Rufus and his brother Robert in Rouen had already broken down and Rufus had set his sights on punishing him.

The next year saw even more varied tasks added to Rannulf's list. Control of the North of England was still a problem for Rufus; a priority to resolve. Rufus had successfully regained Cumbria, including Carlisle, from the Scots in 1092 and the following year had built a new castle at Carlisle to reinforce his defences. But the New Castle on the Tyne was still a simple motte and bailey type.

His hand was forced by yet another rebellion in Northumberland in 1095. Rufus sent a strong force north to deal with it and, in doing so, set out to upgrade the castle, now in the new Northumberland, north of the Palatinate of Durham, to a frontline defence against the Scots and a clear statement of intent to Northumberland's tetchy residents. He confiscated the castle from the custodianship of the local earl, made it a royal castle and started the building of a much stronger stone castle on the Tyne in place of the one erected by his brother Robert in 1080. Just as important, he took steps to transform the area roundabout into a thriving town, Newcastle. He ordered Rannulf to organise the relocation of farmers and skilled tradesmen from Yorkshire to settle the new town on terms that were beneficial to both the King and citizens.

That same year, the Bishop of Worcester died, and Rannulf, with the King's blessing, introduced a new money-raising scheme; the tenants of the bishop's huge estate would be required to pay a 'relief' to the King in order to retain their tenancies. Whilst it was custom and practice for tenants to make a similar payment when their lord died and his land passed to a new owner, it was not the practice with church land as the land belonged to the church, the bishopric, not, for example, the bishop. There was outrage. The scheme was dropped.

The affair of the fyrd and this scheme caused Rannulf to realise that he and Rufus had ventured too far. It was one thing to target the wealthy, within the law but stretching usual custom and practice, quite another to hit some of the less well-off and by more devious methods. The reaction to the trickery with the fyrd and the unprecedented imposition of charges on tenants in Worcester was strong and critical; actions not to be repeated. Rannulf knew that his grandfather and father would not have been pleased; privately he felt ashamed.

Meanwhile, Duke Robert in Normandy had reached agreement with Rufus for a loan of ten thousand marks to fund his participation in the first crusade to the Holy Land. In return, Robert gave Rufus the lease on his land in Normandy, entitling him to act as Regent there during his absence. For Rufus, it was the perfect opportunity to achieve his ambitions without the need for force. But at the same time, it increased the need for Rufus to raise more cash and keep the pressure on Rannulf.

Rannulf's standing with the King, however, had grown with each year of his reign. He had been rewarded well and Rufus had recognised his achievements by appointing him a Judiciar. Rufus's father had introduced this position to help him run the country when he was away from England. From this small handful of powerful, trusted men, he could appoint two to act as his co-regents when absent. Rufus, away in France more even than the Conqueror, had decided to appoint his Judiciars as permanent positions running his government in England at all times. Rannulf was the first not to have been a baron or bishop. It was a significant milestone. He had become Rufus' leading adviser in charge of financial matters and, increasingly, matters of law in any case where land was involved. But he did not get involved in hearing criminal cases.

As a Judiciar, he supported the introduction of Commssions of itinerant justices from the King's court to investigate Royal pleas in the Shire Courts. The move was the beginning of a process of curbing the powers of the sheriffs, a process which would continue for decades to come. Rannulf participated in two such Commissions in 1095 and 1096. Some chroniclers in Rufus' successor, Henry's reign, referred to Rannulf as The Judiciar, similar to a prime minister. But this was not correct. He was one of five, though probably the most effective administrator. The chroniclers of the day described Rannulf as 'The manager of the whole of England'.

The year 1096 turned out to be quite eventful but not all good for Rannulf. He was disappointed when Samson, who had also served in the Chancery as a royal clerk but was still a cleric in minor orders, was appointed Bishop of Worcester. After what had happened during the vacancy, that was perhaps not surprising, but to see him leapfrog into prominence was galling. However, quite unexpectedly in 1096, William St Calais, Prince Bishop of Durham, died. Not surprisingly, Rufus ordered Rannulf to take over the administration of the estate of this important bishopric, whilst delaying the appointment of a successor; but perhaps working to his advantage. Assignments to Northumberland and Durham were not the usual southerner's idea of personal progress! He dared to hope!

Rannulf took over the bishop's estates with his usual efficiency and speed. But he soon came into conflict with Prior Turgot who told him of St Calais' assignment of more lands to the monastery in 1093. But Rannulf could not recognise this arrangement – there was nothing in writing. So Rannulf took over those lands as well as he was obliged to do. But he felt he tried to reassure Turgot that he would allocate the necessary funds from the bishop's revenues to help meet their costs in continuing the construction of the monastery as well as enabling continued work on the cathedral.

But Turgot was well aware of Rannulf's reputation. Their relationship was strained and mutual trust was lacking.

For the next two years, as ever, other tasks were put his way. He had by then sixteen bishoprics and abbeys under his control. He organised the construction of the first stone bridge across the Thames in London. He supervised the building of a new inner wall to protect the newly finished heavily fortified Tower by the Thames. This Tower of London was intended as a retreat for the royal family in times of danger and be used for high-ranking visitors to the King. He also oversaw Rufus' flagship project, the Great Hall of Westminster.

However, life was too exciting for him to ignore other possibilities of a bishop appointment. One possibility, which previously had been on offer several times, was the prospect of promotion via the influence of the Bishop of Winchester. Rannulf had first met the bishop, Walkelin, on his return from Odo's expedition to Durham. Winchester had continued to be at the centre of Rannulf's work ever since, first Domesday and more recently based in the capital city supporting Rufus. Walkelin had been his informal mentor and Rannulf had developed a close relationship with him. Walkelin was also a senior advisor to Rufus and, as Bishop of Winchester, was the de facto Treasurer of England.

On occasions, both Rannulf and Walkelin were co-regents covering the absence of Rufus abroad. Rannulf felt that the bishopric of Winchester, with all its wealth and influence, might be coming his way – or maybe the vacant, now powerful, bishopric of East Anglia based at the new cathedral in Norwich!

But no, none of these was to be. It didn't help that all of the south, west and middle of England, including East Anglia were all part of the Province of Canterbury under the leadership of Archbishop Anselm. Anselm would never support Rannulf's nomination as bishop. Even in 1097, when Anselm's relationship with Rufus reached breaking point, and Anselm was exiled, and the Canterbury estate seized by the king, Anselm retained his position as Archbishop and hence his closeness to the Pope. And so, in early 1098 when Walkelin died, Rannulf was not to be his successor.

The bishoprics in the north of England, originally based on the ancient Kingdom of Northumbria, were part of the Province of the North under the leadership of the Archbishop of York. Anselm was using his influence and power to extend his authority to all of England. Even though he had not yet achieved that, Rufus would tread warily in the North too. The Palatinate of Durham was technically part of the Province of the North but, in practice, the Bishop of Durham accepted no authority from York. Under a Prince Bishop, the see of Durham stood unique and special, and to Rannulf's advantage!

In 1099, Rufus decided the time had come to nominate Rannulf as Bishop, Prince Bishop of Durham. The king needed someone with the right energy, along with organisational and diplomatic skills, as well as being totally trustworthy towards the King. Rannulf's appointment was almost inevitable.

Before Rannulf set in motion arrangements for his wife and children to be with him at his ordination, he needed to manage sensitively his long-standing loyalties to Alvelva and her two sons by Rannulf, the eldest of which was named Rannulf, sometimes known as Ralf. He succeeded in arranging a marriage for her to a prosperous gentleman living in Huntingdon, who contentedly agreed to take on her family and install them in Huntingdon, with his own children. Rannulf would provide for his two sons.

Thus, shortly after receiving news of his appointment, he went to Dover to meet his young wife, their two small boys and his mother. Frankly, he was a little surprised that she had decided to come. She would be in a strange place away from her family and would not like the prospect of living in a colder climate.

They were to live in the bishop's house within the castle grounds. In truth, it was a compound typical of the residence of a high-status person in the 11th century. The focal point was the hall, but there were many other separate buildings, including the kitchen and food store, the chapel, the stables and workshops. The large hall was where the bishop and his family lived. It served as the meeting place for the bishop's official business, receptions and banquets. But it was also a living space. Servants and other staff would sleep on the floor of the hall whilst the bishop and his family slept on a raised platform at the opposite end from the entrance. There was little privacy. An important guest would have slept in this same area too, perhaps screened off. During the day, the platform was cleared and at meal times, the bishop, his family and chief guests would be seated on this platform, everyone else around tables in the body of the hall.

His ordination as Bishop was conducted by Archbishop Thomas (the elder brother of Samson, born and educated in Bayeux) of York in June 1099. Rannulf, as well as Rufus, did not agree with Archbishop Anselm's view that all the bishops should be subordinate to the Archbishop of Canterbury nor that the Bishop of Durham should be subordinate to the Archbishop of York. In his ordination service, he successfully managed to avoid any such oath as had St Calais before him, thereby sustaining the standing of his new position.

Although Celestine was very proud of Rannulf at his ordination, by the end of the year she had started to wish, like Rannulf, that she had not, semi-impulsively, decided to cross the sea and try to make a home with her husband without her parents and with only his mother to support her. She enjoyed the trappings of power, but the bishop's compound was exposed to the harsh cold easterly winds and Celest did not enjoy it. She was also frequently missing Rannulf in the early evening and, by the time Celestine had encouraged the two small boys to bed, she, like they, were exhausted. The elder, hearing his papa coming home set up a chorus of 'can we not see him'. A really leisurely evening for the five of them together for an hour was rare. It was also rare to find a short time when just the two of them could relax together, when Rannulf would often eat a curious, strong local cheese. Celestine tried to get Rannulf to concentrate on his episcopal office and his family friendships, but to no avail as his broader roles both as Prince Bishop and clerk to Rufus commanded much attention.

Although Rannulf was no longer keeper of the King's Seal, he did now have his own seal. As was custom, the seal of the old Bishop, William St Calais, had been destroyed on his death and was now replaced with Rannulf's Episcopal seal, shown in the photograph here.

This impression, attached to one of Rannulf's charters, is the oldest genuine episcopal seal held in Durham. The inscription reads "Sigillum Rannulfi Dunelmensis Episcopi" meaning Seal of Rannulf, Bishop of Durham.

Some years later, whilst talking to one of the chroniclers of Durham, he recounted a previously untold story from when he held the King's Seal. It was in the years after Domesday and he told of a group of discontented landowners who wanted to punish Rannulf for his involvement in Domesday. He was kidnapped in London and was taken by boat towards the Thames estuary where he expected to be killed and his body dumped overboard. But he remembered that he was carrying the King's Seal and he acted quickly to throw it overboard before his captors discovered it and realised its value, perhaps to forge papers in the King's name. He decided to engage the lead kidnapper in conversation and promised him he could name his price if he could persuade his colleagues to return there and then to shore and release him. His captor agreed and took him to his house. Surprisingly, he released Rannulf without claiming his reward. Instead, the man took himself into exile fearing Rannulf might turn him in! True or not, something had reminded him of his pledge to guard the seal with his life.

On August 2, the next year, 1100, Rannulf's world, totally unexpectedly, began to rapidly fall apart. He was beginning to accustom himself to a spouse, the small boys, and the problems they posed, when the drama, accidental or planned, took place. It was not long before Rannulf himself needed to take extreme caution.

Rufus had organised a hunt in the New Forest, close to Winchester. Many of his nobles in England and his friends from Normandy were there. His younger brother Henry was present but his elder brother Robert was not yet back in Normandy after the conclusion of the Crusade. Rufus and his friend, Sir Walter Tyrrell, became separated from the main party. Somehow, Rufus was hit by an arrow and died. Not one person stopped to help and take his body to Winchester. Everyone fled. No one wanted to be a suspect. How and why this happened remains to this day unclear, and unknown. It is the view that Walter Tyrell shot the fatal arrow. Was it an accident? Possibly. But Tyrell was probably the finest shot in the party. Was it an opportunistic conspiracy either to enable the ambitious Henry to claim the throne in his brother Robert's absence, or did Robert conspire with Tyrell to avoid having to repay the enormous debt he would owe Rufus on his return?

Henry immediately rode to Winchester to seize the Treasury, his first step in claiming the throne. A passing forester found Rufus's body and transported it by cart to Winchester. On such a hot day, the burial needed to be conducted quickly, and his body was laid to rest in the New Minster with few people present.

After the funeral, Henry met with the attending nobles and bishops in Winchester Castle to start to build his support for seizing the crown. He was encouraged by the support he was given but realised he may need to offer promises to secure that support. Very quickly, all left for Westminster to meet in the newly built Westminster Hall to continue this process and plan for the coronation. The word went out to all the bishops and senior barons and earls to attend at Westminster forthwith.

Rannulf felt at risk and also feared greatly for his family. With no support from Rufus, his protector, he needed to find a safe place for his family, and quickly, before he left for Westminster. Thank God for his mother's presence and initiative. The small boys flung themselves round their father's legs and he just managed to restrain tearing them off and pushing them aside for greater things! They had to be greeted well and gently in order to fulfil a few of the expectations that had built up. Whilst he realised the need for haste, he could not manufacture it, and procedures either took place or not. At this stage, he could only calmly let things happen. With his family now safe in his mother's care, and having handed over his bishop's responsibilities to Turgot, he left for Westminster.

Chapter 4

Escape to Normandy

Rannulf had developed a strong independence, a trait much admired by Rufus in the work he had asked him to undertake. Nevertheless, Rannulf had to remember that the established king, his protector, had been eliminated, one way or another by device or accident. There was little Rannulf could now do about the matter. Shocked to the core, Rannulf, the most recently appointed bishop, his robes in the newest gloss, had arrived at Westminster Great Hall, the construction of which he had overseen on behalf of the now-deceased king. His eyes passed lovingly over the grain in the worked surfaces of the huge timbers whilst taking time to carefully survey the powerful landholders gathered with Lord Henry to consider and make arrangements for his coronation.

On arrival, he had spoken cheerfully to the younger of the bishops, and politely and respectfully to their elders. He had, with care, enjoyed the position he had slowly started to build up. But it was quite soon to end.

Duke Robert had a firm and witnessed agreement with Rufus that both being bachelors at the time, should either die without an immediate heir, each would inherit the title and lands of the other. It was part of the grand co-swearing that those there gathered, who did not include Henry, had witnessed in the candlelight and would remember their life-long. But Robert was not to hand and Henry was; furthermore, he had already taken control of the Treasury and begun the bargaining to gain support for his bid. Whilst still only thirty-two years old, he was an experienced schemer with a powerful base in Normandy and, in recent years, had allied with Rufus against Robert.

The atmosphere was electric but not with exhilaration. Tension, partisanship, and apprehension ruled. Some did not know which group to sit near, and whether to avoid the ambience of the putative king, whether to creep nearby and remain inconspicuous, or whether, like some, a few, to remain bold in their grand robes. Many of these great landholders held titles in Normandy. They knew that the young Henry was ambitious; resenting even his elder brother's dukedom, whose rights in that kingdom had been confirmed by no other than the Duke Conqueror himself. Why had King William Rufus, an active fit warrior, who had come to some sort of working agreement with his elder brother in Normandy, himself a distinguished crusader warrior, suddenly been targeted – in every sense of the word – and taken from them? And now this schismatic situation was thrust upon them?

Without news from Normandy, they were reluctant to act quickly. What positive action might Duke Robert take now? Robert had borrowed a considerable sum – ten thousand marks – from King William Rufus to fund his successful crusading expedition. Now he was soon to be back in Normandy, and it was still outstanding. Had Duke Robert had a hand in Rufus's fate? He now no longer had to repay the money and Duke Robert was evidently England's agreed heir. They feared the young Henry: but they also feared the prospect of civil war between two brothers both here and across the Channel; a war between the many followers of the aristocratic brothers. The endless and endemic prospect of civil conflict created by the brothers' ambitions, spreading throughout the warring forces, and maintaining itself. No husbandry, no crops, no prosperity for years.

What could they do to postpone action without alienating this undoubtedly capable but aggressive and ambitious young claimant? Or his rightful elder brother? Already in control of the Treasury, Henry could hire mercenaries from the Low Countries within days – hours almost – aside from the possible loyalty of the king's household troops based in different castles in both kingdoms.

In both England and Normandy, might was simply right. But there was also a long tradition in England of royal promises made before and in the course of the coronation. All lordship was a two-way process: lords sought loyal service; men sought 'good lordship'. In England, there was also the tradition of the throne being elective from amongst the royal family, 'election' being a variety of nomination.

Followers could insist on some sworn promises made prior to the coronation and it was this that was now dominating the discussion in the hall, a process started in Winchester Castle a few days earlier. Most people in the Hall had grown accustomed to Rufus's eccentricities, but everybody there, including the church leaders, despised the manner in which Rufus had gone beyond the established customs and practices that governed what happened to property and land in the event of death. Norman practices had evolved from Saxon norms but with one important difference; the Conqueror claimed ownership of all the land and then granted large estates to tenants-in-chief, usually his loyal supporters in battle as well as the bishops in return for loyalty, taxes and a commitment to supply knights and soldiers when needed by the King. Tenants-in-chief could divide their lands into manors and, in return, the lord of those manors would take on commitments to his chief and so on down to the villeins and others working their estates. No one free-born could escape the essence of a contract. But Rufus had broken with the established practices and customs, inventing and imposing new or stretched rules, particularly in the event of the death of a lord. The King had used the information gathered in his father's reign, documented in Domesday, about the annual revenues from land and notions of the feudal tie, to make bishoprics and abbeys pay an annual sum to the Crown when they were vacant and to take in inheritance tax similar amounts from the great landholders. Or, to keep the lands in the Crown's hands, administered by the royal clerks, until an heir reached his majority. Sometimes the Crown found an advantageous arrangement – to the Crown, that is – to marry an heiress to an ally. And Rufus's most effective and trusted enforcer was none other than Rannulf. That same Rannulf who knew his way around Domesday probably better than most other of the royal clerks and whose energy, good looks and decisiveness (it was no coincidence he was nicknamed Flambard) contributed mightily to his success. Rannulf, who more recently, had implemented the much-reviled scheme for exploiting the calling of the fyrd and had required new fines, or fees, to be paid by tenants of the deceased bishop of Worcester in 1096 in contravention of custom and practice for church lands. By 1097, Rannulf had been in charge of numerous abbeys and bishoprics, all held vacant so that the king received the revenue. No less than thirteen royal abbeys and nine bishoprics had endured vacancies.

In Westminster Hall, Rannulf now became uneasy. As the conversations around him continued, Rannulf found himself adding aloud, "such sources are necessary for the regular funding of the new kingdom, particularly to secure and strengthen its borders, land and sea, from the king's enemies."

The nearest faces swung round to listen to him: possibly expecting him to elaborate on his mutterings, which he'd had no intention of voicing aloud. *Execution*, thought Rannulf, *is probably the appropriate word in this situation, or perhaps exile*; but he halted the thought as soon as it flicked uncalled for across his mind. He was not good at hiding his thoughts with an impassive face; he knew it took an unceasing effort: one reason he had found common ground with the King, now dead, was that they could both be straight and practical with each other. And often laugh easily together too, though he did have to be careful with that on occasion.

Perhaps some of the royal clerks could now assert the opportunity to get their new lord to abolish these new and, quite evidently to them, evil practices and, at the same time, get rid of those royal clerks, familiar with the process, who enabled Rufus to carry out this aggressive meticulous policy. Rannulf could not escape the fact that he, more than anyone else in the room, was at the heart of implementing and embellishing Rufus' policies. Though he was now a consecrated bishop, a prince bishop, he was also the former king's clerk and Prince Henry, having sharper eyes than even his royal brother or father for revenue and more able to cast his eye over the figures, must have known that the surplus he had just taken over in the Treasury was in large part the result of Rannulf's work.

On all this, the barons and bishops could be united giving them the upper hand in trying to make a bargain before they acclaimed their new king in the traditional coronation service. And negotiations and drafting of such an agreement might give them time to see how Duke Robert acted, and reacted. They drafted a charter, to be made public and declared at Henry's coronation, which required a solemn commitment to end Rufus's reviled practices and remove 'evil' officials of the Crown. And Rufus's most effective, trusted, and in the eyes of some, most 'evil' official was none other than Rannulf.

As the churchmen and royal clerks were preparing to leave the hall, Prince Henry signalled to the lay landholders to stay for a few moments. He called over four men at arms and told them to follow the churchmen and see that they were safely installed in the Abbey for their deliberations in planning the Coronation, and their basic needs met. Now Henry must negotiate with his barons.

As he left the Great Hall, Bishop Rannulf caught a reflected glimpse of his magnificent attire in the window. He felt exposed and opted to slip out for a moment to change back into his old deaconry robes.

Henry proved victorious in winning over the barons and, absent any claim from his elder brother, The Duke of Normandy, was now set to be crowned King of England. But it was at the cost of a series of promises about the good character of his future reign, promises perpetuated in a charter that turned out to be a precedent for the Magna Carta a century later. In that Coronation Charter, the younger Henry agreed to get rid of numerous of his father's and brother's grasping financial practices.

Inevitably, Henry's hand was forced to make a scapegoat of Rannulf, who was arrested just before the Coronation on August 5, and by August 15, he had been sent to the Tower of London to be confined or 'imprisoned'. There was no trial; no one objected!

But the Tower was not a prison. It was built as a heavily fortified royal residence by the Conqueror. Rufus concluded that the original wooden palisade and bank on the west side of the fortress was inadequate. He'd ordered Rannulf to build a new stone wall inside this palisade so that, along with the repaired Roman wall on the east, the Tower (many years later painted white and thereafter known as the White Tower) would be surrounded by a strong, high stone wall. So Rannulf had the dubious distinction of being the first prisoner … and, in six months' time, the first to escape.

The Keeper of the Tower was acutely embarrassed, nervous, even fearful. His own father had recently died; he had taken big risks fighting alongside the Conqueror and been well rewarded in the estates and privileges granted to him and remained a lifelong friend. Young William Mandeville's loss had been tempered by his expected inheritance of his father's few but strategically placed manors and his Essex castle. But now, to add to his own family crises, the political world in England was broken apart.

King Henry had by now confirmed the Mandeville lands to Mandeville's son; and the constableship of the Tower, too. William was now in charge of two key strongholds. Once Henry had been anointed and acclaimed, the men of England, and that included William, could not but recognise the almost sacral office of an anointed king.

In raising the cash over the last fourteen years, ever since the old king and conqueror had pushed the clerkly officials, and the landholders, to their limits towards collecting the data for Domesday, the clerical officials had become a well-honed team and Rannulf had become the most powerful of all. It was advisable for any great landholder to keep on the right side of this group, and William de Mandeville's father, Geoffrey, had thoughtfully arranged his son's marriage, a happy and quietly beneficial one, with a daughter of Eudo, a fellow Judiciar and whose brother was also a Domesday Commissioner.

Mandeville had recently been so proud to follow his father in office and lands; now he was torn and distraught. It was obviously impossible for William to discuss the situation with his father-in-law, as he was one of Rannulf's closest colleagues: he remembered Eudo and Rannulf had worked together in the Survey on Norwich, travelling amicably together.

Although Rannulf loved moving fast across country, he was also one for enjoying the situation to the full when he reached the host sheriff's castle, seeing what churches, old or now being built, there were in the neighbourhood, and feasting till late in the evening after the day's journey. He seldom lacked energy.

But it was this same Rannulf who was now on his way to imprisonment in the Tower of London, and to the charge of its new constable, William. How was William to conduct himself with such a charge? To add to the irony, it was this Rannulf who, full of charm, and enthusiasm, had told him the history of its building: the very king's clerk who had largely contributed to organising the materials and manpower for the completion of the hall and its surrounding works, just a few years before. It was all a legal muddle too. Until his coronation had taken place, Henry had no authority to confirm William's appointment as Constable of the Tower – only what he had grabbed by the power of possessing the Treasury, and the stability given by the presence of leading bishops. Indeed, Rannulf's predecessor, as Bishop of Durham, although a leading councillor of William II, had argued strongly against the authority of the royal court when it was summoned to judge Bishop St Calais who had stood up to his king and sided with the nobles challenging Rufus on his elder brother's behalf when called upon to aid the king. Rufus had, however, argued that the bishop was there as a landholder responsible for the military troops due from lands to the king, not in the office as bishop.

St Calais had been put on open trial but had only been exiled. Bishop Rannulf had not been tried but he was to be imprisoned in the strongest of royal fortresses. William Mandeville had not had occasion to put his wife to the test like this. As Eudo's daughter with experience of her father's world, de Mandeville was almost sure he could trust his wife to keep her counsel, if he reinforced its import. She might have some sensible words on the practical side at least. His wife had had more than an inkling that something big and difficult was afoot. Now she was appalled as he outlined the dilemma; she was even more aware than he at what might be the effects on her own father.

'Do I treat him like a bishop, with access to the largest room and to the chapel? How *do* I treat him? The grand rooms and chapel were not tailor-made for prisoners. They are for royal security in times of danger and for royal guests. Is he a political prisoner? He evidently is. But they are alleging, pretending, his actions were unprecedented, without the sanction of law or of custom'. He paused. 'Just where *do* I put him? And, either way, what might be the consequences for me?'

Aline, his wife was clear and certain. "You have to, you must, receive him suitably and graciously," she told her spouse. 'Anything other and father would be appalled. Rannulf is still a bishop, has only just been appointed, a powerful one and might well be so again. Will be, indeed is still. The king cannot deconsecrate a bishop: and will have much opposition if he tries to overturn that, or exile him like the previous bishop. Or confiscate the see of Durham's lands. Rannulf is not popular with much of the church, but Samson is an old colleague with a lot of shared memories from Bayeux, as is Thomas in York. You can do no other.'

Rannulf himself needed to be heedful: this was nothing new. Now in the King's custody, he was still in great danger. He remembered from the days of the new King's father that a few of his enemies had been known to die rather mysteriously whilst enjoying his 'hospitality'. But he was not overly concerned about any possible danger in accepting the younger Mandeville's kindness and hospitality during his incarceration though he knew he should not relax completely in his company nor that of his kind and sensible wife. He knew he should not call on his past relationship with William's father-in-law, Eudo. But however much as the hospitality was helping to blunt the painful edge of his sudden fall, he determined to be on the lookout for an opportunity to escape.

William, the new Constable, had a healthy young son, Geoffrey, of whom he was rightly proud. Though he did not bring him often to the Tower, the occasional sight of the young Geoffrey with his father and the chance of playing with him eased the ache, for a few minutes, that Rannulf felt for his own young sons, themselves little more than boys.

William's little boy was usually safely in Essex, away from the wide Thames where the dross of commercial and city traffic was discarded, where the fetid sewage from the city tended to pile up. When visiting William's father's great manor and stronghold there, Rannulf had always taken care to enquire how the young Geoffrey was. What were the two-year-old's latest pranks and words, what curious questions, sometimes cutting to the quick as youngsters' questions did? So, in the Tower, for both men, it kept the focus on mutual and happier subjects, especially, well away from the temptation to voice or even share their thoughts and real concerns.

But at his first encounter with William, when William kindly told him he would treat him as best he could, Rannulf decided to lay some of his needs on the table. 'That is good of you.' Then added, 'I trust I may have my serving boy to accompany me? I fear in the rush of business that I have conducted during King William Rufus's reign – the great survey, roads, bridges, the King's Hall at Westminster, and, completing this very fortress – not to mention the formality required when I was made Bishop has made me dependent on someone's good offices. I have had to dispense with attendant scribes from chapter and monastery who would have been most useful but I do need an alert boy capable of all practical work to keep me looking – and smelling – respectable. He is but a lad taken from the stable and the table in Durham but, in waking and waiting moments, I have begun to rely on him! Rather over-much I fear.'

He waited patiently for William's assent. Eventually, the new constable of the Tower responded, 'I see no reason why not, though perhaps I should add please do not, do not, give me reason to withdraw that!'

Rannulf nodded and thanked him then added with an irresistible impish smile, 'Please, can one of his first duties be to access a draught, or even two, of wine? The fate of my King, followed by my own translation from King's council to imprisonment in my own White Tower has been a shock – to understate the matter.'

And it was through these channels that Rannulf slowly began to put the pieces of his escape plan into place. His intent was to escape back to Normandy, possibly to Lisieux as Bayeux had now been destroyed again by Henry's soldiers. He would escape from the Tower by rope thrown out of the window to enable him to slide down to the ground. The rope would be brought in with one of the regular supplies of wine, and the wine would ensure his guards, again as usual, were soon fast asleep enabling him to start his escape. Getting out through the defensive walls would be easier; after all he, more than most people, was well aware that the defences were designed to keep people out, not in! And any lingering guard would either be asleep or easily bribed. His mother would play a key role in placing the children at a friend's home further along the Thames in Kent, near where the ship was to pick him up and take him to Normandy. Celest would be housed separately a little way off, so as not to draw too much attention to the group. She would travel across the Channel a couple of days later, as shipping was available, to meet up with the family at a handy place.

And so, in mid-February, the plan was put into action. It worked near perfectly. His supporters, as arranged, met him with a horse outside the Tower wall as he dropped from the rope. He was pleased to see his mother with them.

'Ooww. Thank God, Rannulf. You're out of that place. I have it all waiting. The boys are with a couple I know in a lodging close by the ship's mooring. Reliable ... more than. They will defend them with their lives. But first, we'll ride, and at once.'

She helped him onto his horse, seeing he was still giddy from the rope and his fall. He had managed to climb down a good few feet deftly via the rope, and had then lost control of his weight and slithered painfully the rest of the way, excoriating his hands and legs. But the rope was too short, ending about nine feet from the ground, and he had no choice but to let go and fall.

She whispered quickly as they set off, 'Knowing you, I'm sure you've eaten and drunk well enough to last us for an hour or more'; a statement, not a question, rather to reassure herself than to chide her son. Her manservant swung her up into his own saddle. The horses, their shod hooves muffled by a padding of sacks laced closely round them, left slowly and quietly into the shadows. They reached the ship at the prearranged spot on the Kent coast, the children and their protectors already on board. Rannulf made sure that the ship left the English shoreline as fast as possible heading south-east. He gave the captain and his second clear instructions as to where they were finally headed; and joined his mother at the far end of the boat.

'Why Rouen or Caen? Why Normandy? Is that not heading straight for the new king's rival? Will you not be *always* regarded as a traitor now?' Pent up with anxiety, her voice was strained.

'Tch! I served the new king's father, for all the faults in the Conqueror's title and for all his cruelty, well and faithfully; his son King William Rufus, the same; and before that his uncle Odo. Where has that got me? Enriched them in all I did, and without cruelty. I was imprisoned in the strongest fortress in the west of Europe for my care and pains.' He added, "as I know better than anyone, because I organised its completion.'

He started to get heated; he had bottled up so much in the last six months, and now he was with someone he could trust completely. 'Of course, I know the meaning of loyalty: no one better; serving three of the king's family fully and faithfully, certainly not to my own popularity, and, until recently, not to my own reward. But I can offer Duke Robert my skills and, so I have heard, he's much in need of them. Like me, he has put too much trust in that family of his, his own family, and all of them have served him ill. And, unlike me, *he* has even more reason to be bitter, for they are his family, and at bottom he continues to be fond of them, though it has made him far too vulnerable to their protests of brotherly love, combined with their double dealings.'

He added, now cooling down as his mind began to race ahead of his words, 'Now, I want, I think can, put him in a good position relative to the new king whose ambitions towards Normandy and his elder brother's dukedom, I fear, are of over greedy, even evil intent. Despite his seniority, Henry has already deprived him of the kingdom of the English. Never forget! Mamma. The obligation to be a good and loyal lord to your own men is as strong as the obligation to be a loyal and faithful follower. There is such a thing as *diffidatio*. It is a contract; Henry has broken it with me as well as with his elder brother. Well, at the moment, and probably for the near future, I think the inexperienced and arrogant Henry might need me even more than I need him. We shall see. Maybe quite soon.'

He added the last two sentences almost to himself. He knew he could trust his mother with his life, but no other ear must pick up a word on the wind. 'Nor can I imagine that the saintly Anselm will be his unscrupulous servant any longer than a ship can be mustered to safely take him and his clergy out of harm's way. And even the revenues of Canterbury will not hold him in thrall to Henry, when all the facts are known.'

At this last sentence, only muttered to himself, his mother, catching some of it, looked startled and questioning. But Rannulf pursed his lips for a brief moment while giving a slight shake of the head, then continued again, endeavouring to calm himself and reassure his mother.

'You know Normandy and Bayeux is your home, and I see no reason for us to fear the Duke of Normandy. Though he is apt to be gullible, his reputation is of a kind and chivalrous man; even more so since his return from his crusading success.' He added, 'He may also realise what I can offer him.'

He squeezed his mother's arm gently and rested his arm alongside hers. Then ceasing to be totally absorbed with his own matters, he caught sight of his mother's face – totally drained and years older than he had seen before. He was keyed up and despite the pain in his hands, fully alive and on the alert for action. But his mother could no longer absorb any more. Now was not the time for his plans, realising the huge strain and physical danger that she had faced with her characteristic clear-headedness, even though she was now almost an old woman. He saw that, exhausted, she did indeed look frail, and was almost falling asleep as she leant against the lip of the ship's rail.

His own words bit into him – here he was talking about what he could offer the lord of Normandy. It was more than time he offered his mother's consideration and care, and return some of her unqualified love and services. No more focusing on his own situation, at least for now and the immediate future, but he knew he would never change his temperament. He must see her to somewhere she could rest, not disturbing the boys, but close by the youngsters, so that she did not worry how they were. They looked to her as both mother and grandmother, to some extent father as well. Now he must concentrate his energies on the voyage, seeing the three persons most beloved to him safely conveyed to somewhere they all might recuperate and take pleasure in each other's company before he set off to Rouen or wherever Robert himself was to be found.

'Oh Mama, let me see if we can find some rest. You more than deserve it. And I trust we will have landed in Normandy when you next look out. But I must ask you a small favour. Do you have any of the herbal balm you often carry? My one hand would be very soothed by it.'

He gently supported her down to the lower part of the ship with his left hand, putting out of his mind any thought of peeping again at the boys tonight, much as he wanted to. Rannulf's mother was game to take up the offered arm but pride made her unwilling to rely further: they reached the end of the short passage and the 'rooms' which stored ropes and gave overnight accommodation for the moment: one for the youngsters, and one for the two responsible and careful adults entrusted to them, and also the pony. Rannulf's contacts had brought some crumpled bread and dog-eared cheese and also some hand-gathered grass (albeit the grass was now almost entirely brown). The smaller of the boys was almost asleep when he went back to his piles of ropes; the elder instinctively buried himself in his father's clothes and shortly fell asleep there.

Next morning, the boys looked pale and worse for wear. Rannulf was already working out some sort of revenge, except that it wasn't intended as revenge. Rather, he did want to put the current Duke of Normandy, the elder brother, in his right place at the head of church appointments in England; Rannulf did not want to be continually soliciting help for those. He had been given so many prestigious roles in the English church when positions fell vacant, he had begun to take it for granted. That era had gone. But he was still the Prince Bishop of Durham with its great responsibilities and vast amount of land. But even this was now in the balance; he felt in danger of being snubbed and degraded.

Back in August, the boys wondered if they should ever see him again, but it was a short time, only February, before their grandmamma had somehow managed to join with their papa, having arranged some sort of exit from the Tower and rode with him to this ship where they would meet up again. They had just about become accustomed to the idea of their father being in prison in London. And what a prison: probably the strongest in the kingdom! They had been rescued and resuscitated after a rough journey back to Normandy. Their mother and grandmother would meet up soon as Celest, as planned, followed in a separate ship. They had arranged a meet-up by the river mouth, albeit in the bad February weather. More importantly, they hoped to get some land where the young could have as much room as they might wish before settling down each night. But all that was too obvious, too easy. It would have suited Celest and their grandmother fine though not obviously so for Rannulf.

Soon, Celest arrived as planned on another ship, safe and well. The affectionate greeting from his spouse meant everything to him. He put his arm on her shoulders from behind and held it for a long time. He then came round and holding both shoulders from the front, he kissed her forehead slowly. For some moments the world for both of them was unaccountably good. They were indeed oblivious to all else. It was not long before Rannulf found a temporary but secluded home on the outskirts of Lisieux as well as a home for his lawyer friends quite nearby.

Bayeux, like the Liege bishopric, had lost most of its central space during the incessant fighting between Rufus, his allies and Robert. It now needed rethinking again and redesigning. But no one survived who cared for responsibility for Bayeux, and its offices. So, they had instead gone to Lisieux despite there being years, if not decades, of work to make the Lisieux bishopric, now vacant, habitable again for all of them and to create a garden that would provide herbs and food. He had an idea as to how he could secure the bishopric.

Chapter 5

Life back in Normandy

Once the family had settled in their temporary accommodation on the outskirts of Lisieux, Rannulf turned his attention to thinking through how he might approach Duke Robert. He wanted to find out whether any realistic prospects remained open for him or whether he was simply opening the possibility of providing for the two little ones and his wife. He was content to leave Celest with his children in Lisieux, at least until his own notion of ducal service was sufficiently clear.

Rannulf and Prince Henry had no quarrel with each other at the time of Rufus's death. Henry would have been keen to keep him as a top adviser, as he probably possessed the greatest knowledge of the kingdom's wealth and revenue sources, and he was Prince Bishop of the strategically important Palatinate of Durham. But Rannulf did understand that Henry had no choice but to imprison him as a follow-up to the promises made to the barons and the church in his Coronation Charter. The charter, the first of its kind, stated that, '...because the kingdom has been oppressed by unjust exactions ..., I make free the Church of God ... I abolish all the evil customs by which the Kingdom of England has been unjustly oppressed'. A very direct reference to the policies of Rufus which Rannulf had implemented!

Henry had, unsurprisingly, immediately dispossessed him of his bishopric's lands in Durham but he was a little taken aback at the action taken by Archbishop Anselm, who had been reinstated by Henry. Between them, Rannulf also lost his estates and his positions as Master at Dover and Dean at Twynham. Rannulf was no friend of Anselm, the learned former monk. Anselm supported the Pope's reforming agenda. He would not have supported Rannulf's appointment as Bishop of Durham, but at that moment, Anselm had been exiled by Rufus, and Rannulf had been ordained as Bishop by the Archbishop of York, then the former Treasurer of Bayeux cathedral and elder brother of his friend, Samson.

At the St Alban's Court in March 1101, just after Rannulf's escape, Anselm had managed to get Rannulf alienated and deposed by the new Archbishop of York, Gerard, who had only just taken over from Samson's brother, Thomas. A letter to Anselm from Pope Paschal supported this action and specified that he should only be readmitted as bishop if he could clear himself through compurgation; that is the supporting oaths of six fellow bishops. Rannulf desperately wanted to regain his bishopric at Durham not only for himself but for his sons and wife too. But he appreciated the danger he was in and the uphill climb he had to take to regain his standing both in Normandy and England. He was an escaped prisoner of King Henry, despised by the Archbishop of Canterbury, and by many others in the church and amongst the landowning barons in both England and Normandy. That he was a Norman by birth would stand him in little stead here. The exception might be Duke Robert.

Even though she loved the lively life, his mother had counselled him that he had plenty of time now to lose himself entirely from the mainstream of political activity. But she knew from what Rannulf had disclosed to her on his escape by boat that, even now, he was already wondering how to show his face at Court in Rouen without landing himself in more dangerous water than before. Rannulf suspected it would not be long before the younger brother of his royal lord landed an attack on the elder. It was not to his liking but there was certainly no offer from the King's court. He did not want to jeopardise himself in either Normandy or England but his choices were limited.

Despite his concerns, Rannulf had been welcomed back into Robert's court in Rouen and was soon appointed as a senior advisor helping Robert to plan an invasion of England to challenge his younger brother Henry. If his different loyalties became incompatible, he could not help the dilemmas forced onto him by circumstance. But any loyalty he had did not embrace fighting, which he thought of as largely pointless. He had already explained that to Duke Robert and others, though he could not appreciate how far they realised that he did not believe in fighting, but that he only worked for agreements between the two men and their followers.

During these early weeks in Rouen, Celest repeatedly begged him not to do anything that would endanger him or his family and certainly not get him taken abroad again. She had certainly less sympathy for Rannulf's fall than she had had for his incarceration! Her primary concern was for her children. She would have preferred to find a permanent home for them all, but Rannulf's mother counselled her to be patient; "Can you not wait in seclusion until you see the strength of Rannulf's position and whether he needs a hidey-hole, and another escape?"

Reluctantly, Celest agreed. Celest now more settled, Rannulf's mother returned to her home in Bayeux.

But Rannulf had also received an unexpected visitor who had declared himself as a messenger sent by Henry. How Henry had discovered where he was, was a mystery but spies were everywhere and, of course, Henry knew many at Robert's court! It seemed as though Henry was trying to find a way forward to bring him back to England and to Durham in particular. But he could not be sure and the messenger had not yet revealed any quid pro quo for the king's help. The messenger seemed to know that he was now working for Robert, but had so far not enquired about what he was doing. And Rannulf told no one of these meetings; secrecy was essential not least for his own safety. No one knew what the messenger relayed, no one knew what message Rannulf sent back.

At first, Robert's preparations appeared disorganised and Rannulf was able to bring some sense of planning into the build-up. By mid-July, a sizeable army and fleet had already been assembled and Rannulf was well informed of Henry's defensive army as well as Robert's plan to attack England at Pevensey.

These last six weeks had also determined his thoughts and encouraged a new formulation. Rannulf had become the strategist and was now focusing on organising the seaborne operation to depart from Treport. Using his connections in England, Rannulf had been successful in persuading some of the ship commanders in Henry's fleet to make the passage of the English Channel for Robert's fleet possible and free from attack by Henry's own fleet. He wanted Henry's forces to think they would land at Pevensey, but he aimed to deceive them and land in Portsmouth. That way, he hoped Robert's army could reach Winchester and seize control before Henry's troops could discover the deception and scurry across country to prevent Robert reaching Winchester unchallenged.

Celest accompanied Rannulf to Treport, but this was no time for debate. Rannulf could only tell her what would happen when they arrived. A quick look at the ship was all that was permitted. Any attempt at a slight protest from Celestine provoked nothing but the fiercest of looks and a beckon towards the ramp of the ship, without a supporting smile, and only a half turn of her husband's back. It had the required effect. He had a few moments to take in the experience, and then it was gone for the summer. In its place, were major constitutional questions, which could easily have become a matter of life and death for him.

On the ship, Rannulf was revived by the opportunity just to get fresh sea air without present danger, and to talk quietly with Robert in the corner and finalise thoughts. He knew that he was in danger of being sucked into fighting which, with all his heart, he wanted to avoid. His hope and the plan he discussed with Robert was to confront Henry's forces, yes, but engage, no, rather, propose negotiation. Privately, Rannulf needed to make his own peace with Henry, in the hope of restoring his bishopric of Durham.

Despite Duke Robert's plans to sail for the old invading ground of Pevensey in Summer 1101, the fleet under Rannulf's plan would now sail past Pevensey to Portsmouth where his army would land; an army that included mounted troops of various levels including many knights making Duke Robert and his forces ideally placed to move on to Winchester. It was managed in relative secrecy. Less than four months after Rannulf had escaped from the Tower, he was back on English soil alongside a significant force led by Duke Robert, confronting Henry. But Robert paused his advance to give his troops rest before advancing. Henry's forces spotted the danger before it was too late and marched quickly from Pevensey to Alton where the two forces met. Amazingly, quite possibly as a result of Rannulf's diplomacy with both Robert and Henry's messengers, both knightly forces were, somewhat bizarrely, permitted by agreement to do battle with each other **for two hours.** Their respective forces of a thousand or more were given equal weight to tussle it out. A splendid sight no doubt. After two hours neither force reigned supreme. Neither side could win. It was agreed all round to cease action and to adjourn to a more convivial place where the weighty landholders might negotiate a settlement. Both leaders each appointed a team of twelve knights to sit down and thrash out a deal. Rannulf would have preferred to have been part of Robert's team, but that was not possible.

What was agreed was the 1101 Treaty of Alton. In return for Robert agreeing to pay homage to Henry as the rightful king of England, Henry agreed to relinquish most of the lands he had captured in West Normandy and to pay Robert an annual annuity of three thousand marks. It was also agreed that should either Duke Robert or the King die without a lawful male heir, the other should inherit the Anglo-Norman state. Within weeks of agreeing the treaty, possibly in recognition of Rannulf's role in the invasion plan, King Henry issued writs restoring his bishopric estates within the Palatinate and ordering his staff to be reinstated. However, his valuable estates in Yorkshire and that part of his diocese which extended into Westmoreland, instead, were given by the king to the See of York. Several small manors which Rannulf had acquired from bishopric estates he had managed during a vacancy were also not returned; the original occupants had protested to Henry and Henry, not wishing to be seen to be going back on his punishment of Rannulf, had agreed with their case and reinstated their lands.

Rannulf was cautiously optimistic but he was wary of the vagueness of some of the clauses in the treaty. Until his estates and bishopric were more secure, he felt there was a stronger future in Normandy than back in either Hampshire or Durham, more security for his small family whatever befell in the way of ecclesiastical appointments. But it was an important step in the right direction for Rannulf.

Back in Normandy, Robert, in appreciation of Rannulf's advice and help in the planning and execution of his invasion, appointed his brother, Fulcher, as Bishop of Lisieux. He had helped his brother before, having arranged for him to be a minor royal clerk in the Chancery in the latter years of Rufus' reign. Robert could not offer that position to Rannulf because of the

Pope's condition for his return not yet being able to be satisfied. Neither could someone hold two bishop posts in two countries. However, Rannulf was appointed administrator of the bishopric, in charge of expenditure and revenues.

So, by September, he had a working relationship of sorts with Henry. Rannulf knew it wouldn't be that simple and still needed to be wary. For example, he needed Anselm's blessing and he would not get that until he had the support of six bishops. Little attention, as Celestine observed, came from Archbishop Anselm, and what she did observe was worrying. Their marriage, observed and respected in Bayeux, was under question elsewhere as Anselm sought to apply different and new standards within the church, namely that all priests should be unmarried. With his respected legal and monastic background, Anselm was seen as the leading proponent on the matter and of other important changes in the Catholic Church. Most people in England did not know about Rannulf's situation and those who did were keeping their knowledge private. It was up to Rannulf to develop the support of other bishops, especially in England.

With his fortunes slowly turning, he was also awarded in that same year, two prebends, one at Salisbury Cathedral and one at Lincoln, both places where he had given endowments whilst in the service of Rufus. He had been able to retain his position as canon at St Paul's in London where Maurice remained Bishop and to hold the associated prebend of Tottenham. Armed now with some income in England from both Durham and his prebends, in the spring of 1102, Rannulf quietly sailed to Durham to re-establish contact with the monks in the monastery who formed the dean and chapter of the Cathedral. His relationship with the monks was thawing, albeit slowly, with some of them beginning to realise that cash from Durham was being ploughed back into rebuilding the fortified promontory which was their home and not lining the pockets of their bishop or the king. But his relationship with Prior Turgot was deteriorating. Perhaps that was not surprising as Turgot had been overlooked as the successor to St Calais yet had effectively run the bishopric for much of the time since St Calais' death in 1096. But at least both Bishop and his Chapter enjoyed shared priorities for the new cathedral, creating a quiet open space between the castle and the religious buildings, and completing the monastic buildings. One item near the top of Rannulf's desires was the planned translation of St Cuthbert's body to the chancel of the new cathedral.

Having passed on his instructions for restarting the construction of the cathedral, particularly the completion of the chancel, Rannulf made a speedy return to Normandy. Sadly, shortly after his arrival back in Lisieux, his brother, Fulcher died. Despite fierce objections from the church hierarchy in Normandy, Rannulf was able to gain Duke Robert's support to have his elder son Thomas, only just now an adult, appointed as Bishop of Lisieux. Known as the Boy Bishop, Thomas, who was not in strong health, needed his father's constant support not only in his ecclesiastical duties as Bishop but continuing to administer the bishopric as he had done for Fulcher. His fellow bishops were also concerned that Thomas was not in good enough health but they kept their concerns muted. Even more contentiously, Robert had also agreed that if Thomas could not continue, then his younger brother Elias would succeed him. This was exactly the sort of interference in church matters that the Pope wanted to end, but at this moment in time, the church's authority around Europe was weak.

Despite working hard in Lisieux, Rannulf's heart was increasingly now in Durham, spending as much time as he could planning the evolution of the cathedral, the area adjoining, the city fortifications and many other projects. Above all, he was determined to protect the peninsular, the cathedral and Durham's people from future attacks.

He returned to Durham in the summer, 1104, as secretly as he could, by sea, but this time with his wife and two sons. A special ceremony in the now-completed chancel of the new cathedral witnessed the translation of St Cuthbert's body and the remains of the Venerable Bede to their final resting place. The prior and monks led the proceedings. First, they removed the ancient coffin from the old White Church on the other side of the river and took it into the Chapter House before entering the choir. In silence, they opened the coffin to verify all was as it should be. To their surprise, joy and fear, St Cuthbert's body remained uncorrupted. According to the writings of one of the monks present, Prior Turgot had to intervene to encourage his fearful fellow monks to examine the contents carefully, touching and lifting the body momentarily and rearranging the bones of St Bede and the skull of St Oswald which shared the coffin. The coffin closed, they processed through the quire, the place of worship for the monks, to an area behind the altar at the east end of the chancel. There, the coffin would be laid to rest. Bishop Rannulf insisted he also verified the contents of the coffin and afterwards delivered a long, but not memorable, sermon to close the proceedings.

It was a very special occasion not just for the monks and for Rannulf but for everyone in Durham. A proud moment. But for his own safety and that of his family, they soon made ready to leave and return to Lisieux. He took with him on the ship to Normandy four young horses of the small, stocky breed that he had seen before thriving in the Durham area and which displayed similar characteristics to his beloved palomino.

It was this new focus of Rannulf's, albeit in a colder environment than Bayeux or Normandy, which ensured that Celestine had no intention of leaving the environs of Lisieux.

Somewhat angrily, Celestine told Rannulf; "I am not leaving this river valley and my ancient ties at your suggestion. For once, we can feel safe, or at least more on the safer side. Why can we not live together in mutual peace for a while here, in Lisieux, before we start facing the prospect of always wearing manteau to protect ourselves from the cold, as well as all your other enemies. And your enemies seem to grow more numerous daily. Indeed, all the king's enemies seem to become yours as well."

Rannulf felt more than a little insulted; he was conscious of the sting in the tail of both these remarks and felt them unjustified. He returned the resistance and became a little heated. "Whatever happens, I am putting the boys first. But even so I should like to feel that you are cooperating with me and helping as much as possible."

Celest retaliated, "I can't expect to do everything!", she added with quite a lot of irritation.

But then he reminded himself, as was his habit, of the crises that he had not stopped, could not stop evading, even provoking. With Celestine's responsibilities and the physical attendance to both lads, she had not managed to keep up with all the aspects of their care. He had gone too far. His severe look faded quickly.

He reminded himself again where his priorities should now lie. Fortunately, there was no question of being called upon to go to a meeting in England or elsewhere in Normandy for the moment. The elder boy appeared as twinkly as he had always been, but the younger one was clearly ailing. So Rannulf stayed with the boys, happily and easily, but now conscious that what was needed for them was beyond his powers; that was a matter for God. He hoped so much that these muttered prayers were not rising to his lips too late to have a chance of succeeding. The little lad did not need the rehearsed prayers, but sincere and heartfelt ones from him, Celestine, and Thomas. Sadly, however, despite his best efforts, Elias could raise only an occasional small giggle from them. Rannulf tried to get his mother to return to Lisieux from Bayeux. But he was aware of her failing health, especially after the ordeals of his escape and return to Normandy; his mother must stay in Bayeux.

He had been fortunate to have insinuated his own family into an episcopal position here in Normandy. He was going to do his best to maintain that but he was starting to see, as well as to appreciate in theory, that the young sons and wife of his brother Fulcher also needed support. And, as he drew closer to the boys, they appreciated the physical reassurance he could give them. They clung to him, and he realised, possibly for the first time, that to hold close to them as well as his own sons, became irresistible; and he saw no immediate reason why he should not. It was so new to him to have a heart that dictated his feelings.

Whilst his sons played a much more prominent role in his life, his mind was never far from Durham. However, first, he needed to be absolved by pledges from at least six bishops and to then be reinstated officially by the Pope and King Henry. And finally, he needed Henry to exert the authority of his position over the English barons to give him more acceptable assurance of his and his family's safety in England.

In 1105, Rannulf had to concede that Thomas could no longer fulfil his role as Bishop, a view shared by the local bishops. Elias, the younger son, was also not yet well enough to succeed Thomas, as Rannulf had wanted. Until a successor was appointed, it was agreed that Rannulf would stay in Lisieux to continue with the administration of the bishopric.

However, it was also that year that relations between Henry and Robert once again worsened and Henry decided to invade Normandy to secure it for himself. To Rannulf's dismay and sadness, Henry's supporters set fire to much of Bayeux and many buildings, including the new cathedral, were damaged or destroyed. His younger son was distraught.

'Oh, papa! We were certain that you would not permit the burning of Bayeux: those beautiful buildings and windows. And the gardens. We knew you loved the old gardens.'

The elder, Thomas, remembered even more. In the crypt of the cathedral there used to be an unusual statue of the Virgin. It depicted a realistic but ancient-looking Mother and Child. Rannulf learnt that it might have survived the fires above because the heat and the oxygen were low in that dark place below ground. Many of his colleagues in Lisieux had mentioned that several revered figures of the Virgin and Child had gone missing from their cathedral some years back. When he returned to Bayeux to view the destruction, he made a point of searching for the figures. He found them in the crypt and took them back with him to Lisieux. There was much joy earning great respect for Rannulf from far and wide.

Rannulf's achievements in Durham and in Lisieux became widely known and appreciated in England and Normandy. Under Rufus, he had gained credit for surveying the site of a new cathedral at Norwich and arranging for the land to be allocated to Bishop Herbert de Losinga, its founder. And, he had also gained the positions as the senior canon of Salisbury and Dean of the two strategically important colleges of secular canons at Dover and Christchurch (though Henry and Anselm had since stripped him of these latter roles after his imprisonment).

During his visits to England in 1102, 1104 and 1105, he had not only met quietly with King Henry but also built and rebuilt his relationships, and therefore support, with some of the English bishops. Whilst Anselm would never come to like him, some of his fellow bishops in England realised that Rannulf had served his church well. So it was around this time that six of his fellow bishops were able to meet in compurgation, most probably in England, though there is no surviving written record of this, accepting him as part of the church. He prayed for Anselm's blessing and, thereafter, for the Pope's approval.

Once more, Rannulf counselled Robert to sit down with Henry to negotiate a peace; but Robert did not listen this time. After a lull in the fighting over the winter of 1105-6, Henry's forces returned to Normandy, finally defeating Robert at Tinchebrai in late September. Robert was captured and it wasn't long before he was imprisoned at Devizes Castle in Wiltshire. He was transferred to Cardiff Castle where he died many years later. The Bishopric of Lisieux was now in the gift of Henry. Rannulf learned that Henry intended to appoint John de Seez; he knew John and considered him a good choice. He resolved to continue his efforts to sustain the bishopric and help rebuild Lisieux until John arrived and was anointed as bishop.

Rannulf had now lost the support and protection of Robert. He realised that, before the king became his full overlord, he had better remove himself to his diocese in northern England and take up as much as he could of its demesne lands, as unobtrusively as possible. With all the changes in loyalties, losses in war, and in some cases even executions, it would not be surprising, especially with the lowly status given some of his oaths of loyalty, if he were amongst them, suffering from the king's power. He needed to get away as quickly and as quietly as he could to his diocese of Durham. And work as hard, unobtrusively, and intensively as he could there; building the cathedral and making the citadel safe. With winter fast approaching in Durham, he planned to get back to Durham in the Spring.

Rannulf also began to address himself seriously to the boys' future and that of his wife. He realised Celest was not well; she had had all the anxiety. 'My dear one,' he tried to explain to Celestine, 'I'm sure you realise how much I had at stake: life and limb, as well as status here. And the boys, of course; I can't excuse myself, especially to you. I want to get a situation that can reassure us all. Here, we do not now have a position secure enough to reassure any of us. And with all Henry's progeny looking for appointments and favour in Normandy, the prospect here is remote. I am afraid it will have to be in Durham." He tried to encourage an interest in their next move. It was more than six years since they'd shared anything approaching a joint home that he now held up as an aim. 'I know it will be colder, but at long last some security will be there,' he added. 'And I will do my best.'

He held his arms about her to convey his admiration for the practical strength she had shown and to infuse confidence in her. Moment by moment, the troubles of the Duke of Normandy and of the young King Henry were beginning to lose primacy with him, compared to those of Celest.

Over the coming weeks, he tried to find some common, more reassuring ground to build Celest's readiness for the inevitable change. He began talking about gardens they might create describing an herb garden in Durham as he imagined it. Normandy in the eleventh century had already become a land of abbeys with their rich, productive gardens, but not yet England. Despite the chill further north in Durham, Rannulf's imagination and experience encouraged a range of possibilities. He tried to keep the old Bayeux out of his mind, introducing multiple possibilities of flowering and scented herbs, many of them inspired by sheltered sites near the Norman coast, and encouraged Celest to contribute any suggestion that pleased her.

There was little as a foundation in Durham. Mainly nut trees, with some young apples, interspersed with a few old contorted trees. A stone wall or two, and a few wattle fences might quickly provide protection from the north-eastern weather. Foodstuffs such as beans and peas were basics, as were crops, such as onions, garlic, mint, and cumin, all of which grew quickly. Oats were usually obtainable from nearby Durham fields; some purchasable from the peasantry and tenantry. Some constituted their rent. But his wife seemed disinterested.

His younger son seemed to pick up the continuing unease. 'By hook or by crook' he interjected. Elias had picked up the traditional English phrase, and fastened onto it, producing a spontaneous smile of affection from both Celestine and Rannulf. 'Papa, I will help to collect and stack suitable dry firewood and keep my Mama warm'.

"Elias, a good idea. Thank you. But wait a moment. This is important for all us. I'm afraid there will be no more Lisieux, nor anywhere in Normandy, for the Flambard family. I shall have to get to Durham, get the habitable buildings completed and the garden begun. I will have to leave it to King Henry or his agents to give consent as quickly as possible."

He added to himself, "... and permission to keep mind, body, and family as safe and as long as possible."

Rannulf also confessed to Celestine that he had made a payment of one thousand pounds to the King which the King had graciously accepted. Such payments were not unusual as would-be bishops sought the nomination of the monarch. But in this case, the King had not demanded it, rather Rannulf had volunteered it, realising that he remained vulnerable to being the escaped prisoner, still not formally forgiven, not pardoned. It was a small price to pay for making his own position as a free man and as a Prince Bishop more secure and on a formal footing. Celest was pleased he had shared this confidence with her.

Celestine, despite her illness and despite her dislike of Durham's cold winds, could not but welcome the practical turn matters had started to take. With the better weather of springtime approaching, Rannulf would make his arrangements as speedily as he could. He did not want to remind her again of this: she was too bright to be 'nagged', and evidently now too poorly, too. He gave her a long, slow wink, followed by a long, slow kiss over the eyebrow and he could see that his meaning was understood. He backed out of the family group and promised to be back for supper.

At supper, Elias said, 'I want to come with you. Can I?'

'Maybe' said Rannulf, 'if Thomas is content with that'.

'But Papa, you haven't really been properly appointed, have you? You haven't fulfilled what you intended? Have you got all your Durham lands and military posts back?'

'Indeed, I have. However reluctantly, Archbishop Anselm and the Pope have agreed to my reinstatement as Bishop. The King has agreed to my role as Prince Bishop too. The lands are restored though sadly not fully. With time, we will be able to make things work and be safe.'

'So can I come with you?'

'One day soon, if you get yourself well, you can come and help me sort out the land while Thomas helps Mama and Grandmamma here. But you must get yourself strong first; otherwise, I shall be in the doghouse.'

'Try to sort out some ideas about a herb garden, perhaps with some flowering herbs, which are also tasty ones. We shall have to start virtually from scratch when we get there.

'And we must be ready to leave quickly once I get notice of the better weather to sail north.'

The prospect gave the boy exhilaration and the feeling that, at last, the world was opening up a little to them all as soon as they could get well and start to flourish. Like his father, he had to try and forget the consequences for their Lord Robert of losing the battle with Henry, rather try to progress by succeeding themselves elsewhere!

Now he had made the promise to the lads, he felt obliged to stay at least a week to see how well his sons, and his wife, sustained themselves, and if the younger boy could feasibly accompany him. He surprised himself by finding how much he was hoping this would happen. Elias was obviously keen. The following week, plans had been made. Rannulf explained to Celest his hopes. She was the only one of the three who seemed to have weakened in the interval. He found himself more than anxious on leaving her and explained to her at length what their separation now meant to him.

Chapter 6

Time to Leave

'Papa, you can see for miles from here,' the young boy said excitedly. 'But it does look hard soil to cultivate. Do you really think you will be able to do it?'

'I shall, as usual, do my best, and leave the rest to fortune. One can't usually do much more.' And he smiled and winked at his potential helper and added, 'But this time, of course, I will have you to help me.'

The sight of Durham did not revive him immediately. He was tired. He pulled himself quite sternly together, and made himself realise the possibilities. Although the elder son was getting stronger, he had worried about his wife succumbing to the boys' illness. She seemed tired and drawn when he had left Normandy and would not have fared well if she had to battle it out with him on the cold, easterly-facing slopes of the peninsula. He needed to find a more protected position. The Bishop's Hall, where they stayed this time, was perfect as his official residence, but for his family, especially Celest, he needed to find a smaller building better protected from the elements and, in the longer run perhaps a home off the peninsular to the west.

The old stables were important to Rannulf as a more private base, and he did not see anything better for the moment. There were two good stables, made of four or five stalls, or at least several stalls and one shelter for hay. Flambard saw one upper room which would give him the seclusion he needed in his planning. The heat of the afternoon sun intensified. The stables were quite cool and Rannulf insisted they were kept tidy and quiet, and his old mare similarly. It was his son who started to get clearing and confidently earn accommodation as a groom and even started to enjoy the rather temperamental creature. One thing he regarded as certain, he was going to maintain the little blonde horse, or as near as he could of her type, as long as he remained bishop. When he returned with his family, he would bring the four horses he had been training at the bishop's stables in Lisieux.

He had told his family that he expected them to treat his old horse with respect. They had seen something of the aged horse during their time in Normandy, and they had begun to know what Rannulf meant. They had seen the suffering of several of the knights' horses, some too badly injured to recover enough for any active life, whether as a mount for a knight or to pull a cart loaded with equipment. In battle, there was only one solution for such a horse, and that was to call the knacker who usually accompanied the army; he had two strong arms and a sharpened axe, and the result was distressing. But their injuries had no sway with the two boys, rather the reverse. They spent much time trying to restore them again to good health and put to light duties. Elias especially had begun to appreciate the horses themselves, and to work hard to ensure that they succeeded.

That first evening, Rannulf and his young son were invited by the monks of the monastery to eat with them in the refectory. It was an important occasion; he needed to establish good working relationships with them not only as the chapter of his church but also as an important ally and supporter in his efforts to build the new cathedral and improve the security of the town. He took a small swig of wine before heading over to join them. The monks from an early time had distrusted Rannulf's plans and motives even when he was appointed bishop in 1099. Since then, a few of them had begun to appreciate that, as bishop, Rannulf would live frugally (save for buying a good supply of wine that he would share with his monks!) and plough back the remaining surplus into funding the building, not only of the cathedral but improving their monastery and the peninsular town. Becoming a more harmonious team would take time and Rannulf had to set the pace.

So, the evening meal itself took on, after a little negotiation, a sort of significance of its own. Rannulf had got on surprisingly well with most of the monastery's community though the Prior, Turgot, remained remote, distanced. During the evening, he had managed a little time alone with Turgot in an attempt to build bridges. But Turgot told him that he thought it best for them to part ways so each could start afresh. Turgot had developed close ties with Scotland in recent years and was aware of the vacancy of Bishop of St Andrews. Rannulf offered Turgot his support for his efforts to be appointed.

After a hard day's work, Rannulf and his son took bread and soup and beer with the monks most evenings and, like this night, Rannulf fell into bed afterwards. But he was careful to arise early and start to work on the buildings. That way, he could show his keenness, without making much of a display of it, and it encouraged his son to do likewise with the garden and the horses.

After that first night, Rannulf ensured that the youngster sought out his monastic gardens and plots, encouraging him to come up with ideas without expecting a miracle. Rannulf was no gardener. Oh, that his mother was here! But Elias was enthusiastic. Rannulf readily agreed to some of his ideas but was reluctant to throw ideas out. He gave himself a day or two to try to improve them even if only to alter a plant's position. Both boys thought highly of mint and even then, Rannulf was able to supply several possibilities, especially the names of those mints flourishing best in shade. His own favourite was apple-mint; it was fragrant but less strident than the strong spearmints. Elias also concocted a mix of the commoner herbs and planted them. They could always chop them off at the root if they found there were too many for now, bake them slowly, and store them. And although Durham was cold, once the herbs had protection, their stores could benefit extensively from those grown in the garden.

Initially, Rannulf concentrated on the cathedral. He wanted to complete the plans for the nave, which had barely been started. Though the external fabric of the Chancel was thus far completed, the church longed for the completion of the nave. The whole was an extremely important new building with novel stone construction for the ribs of the ceiling of the side arcading, redolent of Jumieges, very elegant, and something that was new this side of the Channel.

More importantly, before he left for home in late spring, he wanted plans for the completion of the interior of the chancel through the winter to be finalised. He already had a fine master craftsman on site but his immediate priority was to work with him to identify the additional skills needed and recruit locally where possible and quickly. The response was as he had hoped and prayed. Soon, he had three more master masons on-site. They were comfortably resident in movable lodges of well-crafted wood. Rannulf had been fortunate to pick up the services of the master masons, and he did not intend to let go of them easily; they had great value for him and his precious Durham, even if their presence would prove only temporary. He suspected their very presence was more than a little due to the King having a surreptitious influence on where they went and whose project was forwarded fastest.

The quarrying, transportation and stacking of stone needed to be stepped up. Again, the necessary crafts and labour responded to the call. The stone available in the nearby quarries was what many skilled men called 'freestone': that is, it readily responded to cutting freely to fit in one if not two directions. The masons were responsible for the selection of stone and its shaping for each of the many projects in hand.

When Rannulf was on site, it was surprising how fast there was progress and the quality was high. His organisational skills and clear, speedy decision-making were much appreciated. None more so than by the monks who had initially feared that this increase in activity would lead to a lessening of attention to their domestic buildings.

Rannulf soon had to turn his attention to finding a place suitable for his family and to refurbish the stables in the corner of the castle yard. He had been lucky to find amongst the ruins of the past two good small stone houses; both houses had slate roofs and not the typical thatched roof, which had probably contributed to the destruction of many other buildings. He brought in some of the local house builders supported by some of his bishopric staff to help with the renovation. One of the houses would be for his family's use until something more specific for their needs was planned; the other would be for his chapter's use. The speed and quality of work, as well as their appearance, had delighted most of his monastic community in a way he had not expected.

Time was flying by and Rannulf desperately wanted to start work on what he regarded as the two most important new projects that had become part of his vision for the peninsular. Firstly, he wanted to clear the area between the castle, his official residence, and the new cathedral. Secondly, he wanted to renovate and expand the penisular's defensive fortifications. He spent time with his architect in developing his ideas. The scheme for the rest of the promontory needed fast decision and almost immediate action; it would take many years to complete and could not wait for work on the cathedral to be completed. But, reluctantly, he concluded that work on both these projects should be delayed until he and his family had moved here permanently later in the year. The monks were relieved as they feared the impact these new endeavours would have on their own buildings and projects. Equally, though, they were beginning to appreciate that Rannulf was a man of many talents. Belief and trust were growing.

With the mason, architect, and the reeve, much was ready to discuss; progress was decidedly fast: more than that, it was deeply satisfying. But there was a constant worried ache circling around whatever he tried to do. He missed his family. He had had no experience of this before, and found the lack of concentration disturbing. So, he made every effort to get home to his family as quickly as he could.

It was amazing to see the progress they both made in Durham. He intended that they be ready to return to Normandy within a fortnight, but two tasks needed to be completed before they left: first, the planning for work in the chancel over the coming winter period, and second, the gardens.

Past the first day of November, when the first winter frosts would come, stone laying outside would stop as the mortar would not then be able to set. Likewise, the monks would probably cease their ancillary efforts on outside activities as well as on their residence once the weather closed in. In preparation, Rannulf was anxious to hear every opinion, most especially those of the greatest experts, the master masons, who were listened to as intently by the Durham apprentices as their own assistants.

The talented masons and their craftsmen had produced a magnificent response, and the chancel continued positively. Whilst they and Rannulf knew there was plenty the craftsmen could offer undercover in winter, Rannulf realised that a detailed plan of what needed to be done must be agreed upon so that the necessary preparation of materials could be completed in time. The most important winter project would be to fabricate and erect the permanent shrine to St Cuthbert and St Bede that would both guard the tomb and allow clergy and citizens of Durham alike to pray there without disturbing the worship of the monks in the adjacent choir area. The finest stone had already been reserved for this project so close to Rannulf's heart.

What defeated him briefly was the thought of the garden. He really did feel in need of an expert to design and construct the environment. A small garden could be sited within the cloisters. But he needed to find a larger plot further from the church, where he could later perhaps build a new house for his family and develop a large garden – somewhere that was sheltered from the cold east winds – somewhere he and Celest could walk in quietude – and the youngsters could too if they behaved appropriately. But all that was a long way, or at least some way, off. There were many things to consider; not least the soil needed to both grow the basic vegetables as well as herbs and flavourings such as horseradish, leeks, and onions. It also made him realise that there were other herbs, not a few introduced from Italy or Europe, which fulfilled many functions and made the product delicious. Celestine had expertise where he did not. Ideally, he wanted his wife to be part of that process, but he felt compelled to make a start now. At least, however, surprisingly and reassuringly, he felt that the soil now seemed to welcome him to this area; whereas the earlier atmosphere had been one of cold rejection.

He asked his reeve to find a knowledgeable gardener he could meet with the next day. Overnight, Rannulf might have thoughts of where it might be placed. It seemed that at least two sorts of garden might be opportune – a dry stony base would be suitable for Mediterranean plants and a deeper, richer patch suitable for English vegetables. They amounted to many options in all. The following day, he met with both the reve and the gardener and felt happy to leave the task in their hands until he returned in a few months' time.

He planned their sea journey back to Normandy in the next day or two. He intended to break the journey at Lincoln for a couple of days to allow him time to sit with his fellow canons at the cathedral there. Both were ready. His son had managed to finish preparing the soil for a garden for the monastery. All looked much neater, with some plants in the ground ready to go, but he knew how easy it was for those doing the building to ignore the previous efforts at laying out a garden, and the whole thing to become trampled in their absence.

'If I can manage it,' he said to his youngster, 'I will make use of this time, to visit Lincoln, to check all is well with my fellow canons and then head for Dover. We will do our best to meet up with Mama as soon as possible. I know we are both restless and anxious to get back.'

He also needed to check on his small horse, making sure she was fit and well and had a companion to share the load. She had adapted slowly but well to the conditions in Durham and he had been able to enjoy an occasional good canter to get away from his obligations within the episcopal family.

'Papa, would it be a sensible idea for me to try to plant some flax and also some hemp in a couple of sheltered places, the linseed especially. We will need some material for practical articles. It could be made into ropes, fishing lines, bow strings, and other useful bits and pieces.'

'Excellent idea, but be sure to get it done today,' said his papa.

The next day, they left for home together rather content with their achievements.

'Oh, papa, it has been so good working alongside you: I didn't know how satisfying it might become. I do hope Mama has survived the absence well, and I look forward to seeing Thomas again. Papa, we have had such a struggle to try to get well again and to live up to your efforts to help us. First Thomas, and then me even more. We thought we were coming to the end of it all. Mama tried her hardest to keep us in those appointments at Lisieux, but we could see we were not popular with the other clergy, however hard we tried. And Thomas tried even when I did not, even though that sort of learning does not come easy to us. It was so much nicer to be just part of the community, as we were sometimes with our grandmother in Bayeux. And now, first our grandmother, and now our Mama are not well. I think it is the same trouble as we had last spring, but we are getting better now. But I do worry about her and my brother, and my grandmother and you.' He added: 'And Mama could do with support from us all.'

Rannulf's young son's words stung him. Rannulf felt guilty and depressed but his son unexpectedly changed tack and added, 'I suppose you will soon be giving thought to your old work in Lisieux.'

'Don't worry about my work young 'un; you should know by now that my work changes all the time. But I'll survive. The point is, it will be so good to be all together. First of all, I have to give priority to your Mama.'

A few days later, back in Lisieux, Rannulf and Elias were greeted first by Thomas. 'Papa', rang out as the little palomino mare with Rannulf atop came into the yard. 'Steady, steady,' was the mantra that greeted him. Yet it was kindly in tone, and only came as a reminder that Rannulf's small horse was temperamental even if well-taught. Once those on foot were aware of his mount's liveliness, he managed to swing off the mare and concentrate on his sons, whom he quickly found meant more to him than he had ever envisaged. Hearing the hullabaloo, Celestine, realising Rannulf had arrived back, came out into the yard. They all greeted each other warmly. But it was the greeting between Rannulf and Celestine that made them all realise the significance to themselves and their family. Celestine was still evidently unwell, but it was clear how much the brothers and Rannulf meant to her, and how much their return made her happy.

The boys could now look forward to a more stable and secure position in England, and Celestine herself felt more secure. Rannulf's position in Durham gave that sense of security. It clearly meant a good deal to Celestine, and she hoped it would soon mean a great deal more.

Both sons made themselves as pleasant to their local community as they could, and quietly tried to fit in obediently with their parents. Both were obviously maturing although there was some way to go before they were given independence, and the last few weeks had made a difference. Rannulf had several stories to tell her about their activities at the cathedral construction site, with the architect, and downstairs in the stables with the horses. He checked with his family on their progress in training the four young horses that they would take back with them to Durham; one for each of them. He gave them instructions to step up their training and riding.

Celestine was wholeheartedly glad to receive back her youngest son, but most of all, Rannulf. She had obviously been nervous about the extent of time of the break and, again, the way the break in domesticity might detract from their closeness. But there was no question of the latter. Rannulf was happy to use his domestic stamina in a practical way, for once looking after his wife, and remaining as close to her as it was possible to be.

Now, after one full day back, Rannulf wished to escape back to England carefully and safely, keeping a low profile. He wanted to leave as soon as he could, but when they were well enough. But he had spent the first day with his arm around Celestine, talking where they could, planning where they could, their new facilities at Durham.

Rannulf was not nervous of wild surroundings, rather the reverse. He could not help relishing the background of his new professional role as an administrator within the Durham diocese; in some ways, the wilder the environs, the better. He especially loved the drovers' long ways across the moor and the wide and refreshing vision it gave him of future grazing lands and of the seascape. The real shock came when, newly landed in Normandy, he realised that his wife Celestine was certainly not getting better quickly. He now felt uneasy, more than uneasy, about their ability to all get away to Durham in the near future. And his innards palpitated unhappily along with her prospects. He kept visualising a happy Celestine at home with the family and wished he had started preparing the diocese for the family much earlier, or at least that his efforts to bring them all together had not been so diverted and made difficult by the force of circumstances of politics, battle, and to some extent, personalities.

'Oh, Papa', said Elias, 'Mama is not getting any better. I had so much counted on all being together soon. What can we do? Is there anybody that will respond? You know so many learned people. There must be someone who can help and where we can go to seek information. I can ride anywhere now. I will do anything you ask!'

'That's kind. Thank you. I can't think of anyone in the vicinity at the moment. But that's just the kind of action that could prove useful at a moment's notice. Meanwhile please help Thomas sitting with your mother. She would appreciate that. And I would too. Ask her if there are any of her old friends she would like to see soon.'

Four days later, Celestine died. They could not believe how quickly she had begun to dissolve out of their life, changing them overnight from solicitous carers to people who had become merely caring neighbours. Rannulf could not do enough for them but there was little in fact that he could do apart from rearrange their meals, which they had ceased to want, and to contact Celestine's mother. The boys could only remain in charge of simple tasks, and try to give some sympathy to the grieving Rannulf. Thomas had become the more self-contained of the two but his younger brother was the more visibly emotional and distressed. Both boys were certainly deeply affected.

In the last years, many shocks had seemed administered to Rannulf, and now the one occurred most deep-seated of all. One totally unlooked for. He had blundered about in half a dozen spheres quite successfully, but he had not looked for nor received comfort from the Church for this. And he now realised that the successive incidents had been nothing but trauma for his poor wife, as well as for him and his children. The three of them could now only cling together. He knew they would have to move to Durham soon.

Rannulf thought the best thing was to hold a memorial service for her burial and then to move permanently to Durham. At least it would be a different context for his sons, with the different youngsters of the families of masons or small landowners. It was a matter of them all bearing out the predicament, praying, and trying to look forward. How he wished that Celestine could be with them in Durham, creating a home, criticising acutely, yet an integral part of the family with her own strong yet soundly-based opinions.

The year 1106 proved to be another pivotal year in Rannulf's life. His episcopal options in Normandy were now at an end with John de Seez due to be ordained bishop in Lisieux and Richard, Samson's cousin, recently appointed by Henry as the new bishop of his beloved Bayeux. There were no prospects now for either him or his sons. His patron and protector in Normandy was gone, imprisoned in Devizes Castle, and Henry was rapidly putting his appointees in place to secure his grip on Normandy. And worst of all, his Celestine was now gone forever. Durham was his destiny and Henry clearly wanted him there too. There was little they could gain now from Normandy apart from holding their memorial service for Celestine at home and another service when they returned to England and practicalities were less chaotic: a service carefully thought through in Durham.

With all that had happened, they were not ready now to set sail before the winter. By spring, they were ready to leave for Durham. They would sail from Bayeux so that they could say farewell to his mother.

Chapter 7

Prince Bishop of Durham

Rannulf encouraged his mount up the planks and onto the ship. As usual, she followed him obediently but sniffing and snorting at the planks with distended nostrils, rolling her eyes when she felt the rock of the sea beneath her feet, showing the whites first one side of her face then the other. She was always nervous and he had to admit that he too often felt so even though he had done the journey almost as many times as she.

'This will be the last time old girl, I promise.' he whispered, waving away help from his young servant before tying her up, quite short, but not too short, so she had some support. He rubbed her forehead for a few moments, cupping her ears in his hands, stroking them gently upwards with the lay of the hair; and gently stroked her muzzle with the back of his hand.

He whispered, 'I can't ride from Dover to Durham any longer and I couldn't bear it if the journey killed you, so this is the best and quickest way, God willing. I'll give us both a few days to recover when we reach land, and together, we'll arrive in style to our last home in Durham.'

After the mare was secured, his other younger mares, all of similar type and character, were brought on board ready for the journey.

He remembered a recent disturbing dream in which he had looked on these last arrangements to settle in Durham, as their bishop and curer of souls, as something almost akin to imprisonment. But he had banished those thoughts, reassuring himself rationally that few men would consider the diocese of Durham, its monks, its cathedral, its tolls, fortifications, and city to be small confines, especially with his game little mare always waiting in a nearby stable. Now he realised just how much arranging his affairs and getting to the coast had deprived him of his usual energy, both mental and physical. Now nothing more held his thoughts than wishing to get himself, his sons, and his mare safely to Durham.

After arriving in Durham with his scribe, stable lad, his faithful old mare and four of her sturdy kind from Normandy, Rannulf was ready that first morning to get to work. His priorities were to ensure the building work on the cathedral was progressing to plan, to ensure the gardens and demesne lands were productive and that his sons were settled.

Reassuringly, the monastery exuded a sense of quiet industry. Three essential constituents of Benedictine life were liturgical prayer, private prayer and reading, and manual work. There was certainly no lack of the essential manual work conveniently catered for some distance from the main buildings of the cathedral. Close to the east end of the church, near the Chapter House, in a quiet position, was the infirmary for old or infirm monks. Those who had let blood often or recently had their own courtyard and usually appreciated the offer of reading. Next to it was the infirmary garden planted with medicinal herbs. Beyond, the fishponds in the process of being constructed were the orchards and other plantations within the demesne's outer wall. And there was an area earlier cultivated as a herbarium just west of the Chapter House. Nut trees were particularly prized here in the north to shelter and protect plants grown in the monastery garden as well as to provide a nutritious source of food. A new pomerium, a narrow strip of land traditionally laid out to mark the boundary between the buildings of the cathedral and monastery from the rest of the town, was planted there to supply replacement trees to succeed any suffering apple trees.

The boys had now reached sixteen and fourteen years. And they were profiting quite naturally, and directly, from the old apple trees belonging to the outer regions of the demesne of the diocese of Durham. They had also determined to give Rannulf something of a talking to, insisting on him accepting some physical help from them.

'We were talking about it together. We really do want to see some of those marvellous gardens that we saw once in the Loire, and much more often heard talk about. Here we don't mind having a go at the digging – and the planning – if it comes to that. We have unexpectedly found a good nest, which turns out to be hiding away many of the tools.'

Rannulf responded: 'You can't expect just to sketch a garden here with only my or my verderer's permission. It's more than a matter of aesthetics to determine a garden's shape, or view. There is the convenience necessary to the kitchens: the fertile soil necessary to produce fertile vegetables and a rather different soil needed for the fruits; and the right periods and shelter to protect the fruiting in the autumn and the winter. Certainly, a lot for us all to think about and speedily.' His words fell cold and flat on his two boys. Their formality gave them the strength of a distant alien. Rannulf sensed this almost immediately; and decided to start again.

There followed a silence in which Rannulf simply put his arms round the nearer shoulder. He was doing some serious thinking, but unexpectedly, he simply rejoiced in the proximity and the safety of his two sons.

Various breaks in the old levels of the turf signalled the places once cultivated. Some were patently too restricted. The great abbeys he knew in Normandy all had established gardens although any new designs in the garden demanded new shapes and prospects. New cellarers, even new gardeners of different levels would, sooner or later, demand the ability to reshape and to make their own contribution to the grand plan. Between them, the gardeners had to supply the entire house with food and drinking water: for the water could not be guaranteed pure and would need brewing into beer or cider to sanitise it as well as to make it palatable. Every monastery grew some varied-flavoured herbs and individually concocted their own patent gruits to make the taste of the ale acceptable: weak for breakfast, stronger for later consumption in the day, particularly on feast days. Eventually the strengths or qualities of the brew were signified by the number of crosses they displayed on their barrel. It was all to look forward to.

The West range would belong to the cellarer, who was responsible within the monastery for food supplies and the cooking. Ideally it would have a small garden of its own attached to it, growing fruits and vegetables.

'You two ought to have picked up a few tips and ideas in Lisieux before the bishop's house and gardens there suffered in the civil wars. But, of course, at your age, I would have taken little interest in the gardens' fate – the stables were of more concern to me. We are all different, thank the Lord. And given he has somehow saved our bacon several times, we are very lucky. Anyway, it means, whether Lisieux or Durham, there is a lot to do. Share your ideas with me tonight after we have eaten,' Rannulf added with a smile, looking at the apple cores as the boys finished. 'Anyway, it seems that whatever else is catered for, some space must be found for apples good for eating.'

'And me, I should like to try to grow one or two Warden pears in a propitious spot against a wall or hedge somewhere, just in case they can be reared for cooking though, of course, you know that where we are here is a great deal colder than where pears are grown in Normandy. We'll think more about it tonight and put it together tomorrow,' he said simply and reassuringly. 'That reminds me … have you enough straw and blankets to survive tonight? It's all fresh.'

As the following day wore on, he continued to give the two 'gardeners' every respect as he found that their ideas demanded nothing less. They were not equal with the master masons at anticipating the weather but they surprised even the locals with their ideas. They all hoped that soon they could shortly provide the ongoing drinkable liquids and food. However, he or they might be fortunate enough meanwhile to find and buy basic vegetables and herbs from local farmers, perhaps purchasable from those who had small properties outside the city or who knew of caves not too far distant where root vegetables or grain might be temporarily stored. But he needed the gardening plans ready so that they might go ahead immediately with the planting needed for the coming season's supply.

On this second day, Rannulf resolved to begin planning his next steps for the cathedral construction and the rebuilding of the promontory.

An immediate priority was to clear the marketplace place, which separated the cathedral from the castle compound. The marketplace, a hotch-potch of stalls, small houses and other buildings, was unsightly and smelly, and the numerous thatched-roof buildings also presented a fire risk to the new cathedral. He wanted to move the market to the populated flat land to the north of the promontory just outside the dry moat defence surrounding the castle grounds. The monks were delighted and work proceeded apace.

This work had to proceed hand in glove with the building of new replacement homes and a marketplace on the flat area just north of the boundary moat below the steep slopes of the castle. This area would link much better with the agricultural lands to both east and west on the opposite side of the river from the peninsular, particularly when the stone bridge planned at Framwellgate was completed.

Rannulf was indeed 'impatient of leisure': not an easy companion for anyone who had nothing urgent on his schedule, that is, of course, apart from the building of Durham Cathedral and the re-building of its city.

Rannulf, also wanted to improve the structure of the roofs of buildings in other parts of the town, as he had done earlier when preparing the two old damaged buildings for himself and the monastery. The fire risk from using straw to insulate the roof was seared on Rannulf's mind from his experiences in Bayeux and Lisieux, as well as remembering the damage done in the 1079 siege which had first brought him to Durham. He couldn't do it all, but he could provide help to others to achieve this goal especially by providing better transport to bring the stone and slate from the quarries to where it was needed.

He was pleased with the work in the chancel of the cathedral over the past winter. Skilled craftsmen had been brought from as far as they would travel; many knew each other from other projects; several mentioned Pershore Abbey. They had all wanted to work on the shrine to St Cuthbert and St Bede so it had not been easy to assign people to all the different jobs. It took time to evolve, but Rannulf had become widely and even affectionately respected by many of his craftsmen over the years as well as other offices of the church, particularly Salisbury, Lincoln and London.

Beyond these steps, Rannulf's fertile brain was already formulating his big plan to fortify the whole of the promontory with a protective wall around the whole site, including the new settlement north of the castle where the new marketplace was now located. He also wanted to build a wall from the motte to the east end of the new cathedral that would separate the castle compound and the new open space from the buildings on the east side of the peninsula to create a quiet space between the castle and the cathedral suitable also for special gatherings. But all this was a major project, and he would need a lot of help from both architects and builders, as well as the support of the monastery and all the residents. He got that, but the project would require his life's work to complete it.

To complete his vision, he wanted to build the first stone bridge over the Wear just as he had done for William Rufus over the Thames in London. It would be on the west side of the castle to provide a strong entry to the fortified town resistant to both floods and invaders. The bridge, the Framwellgate Bridge, along with a strong defensive gatehouse, was completed in 1116. His accomplishment is shown schematically in the diagram below.

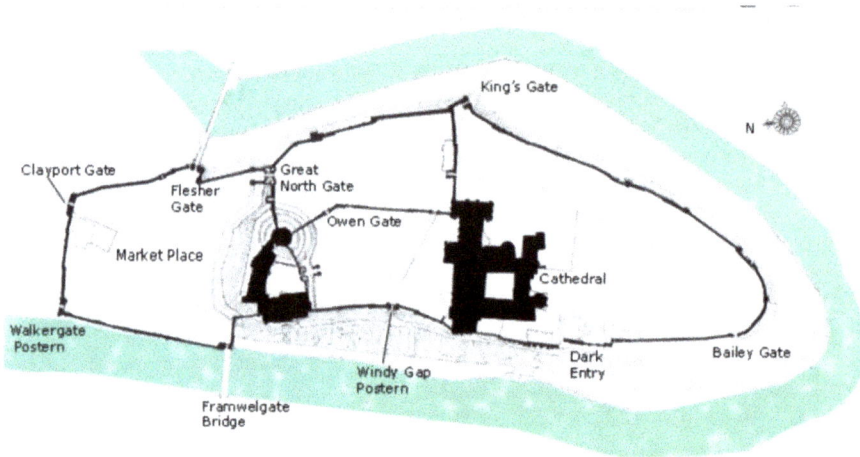

Rannulf's third and most personal priority was the welfare of his two sons, Thomas and Elias. Just as Rannulf had done as a boy in Bayeux, both boys remained at home for some time. They were slow to learn their languages, but both learnt from Rannulf, and also from the monks, even when he was away on the King's business in Normandy. Elias looked after the stables and helped in the gardens and fields, whilst Thomas helped his father with church affairs in the diocese. Rannulf set out also to make some sort of home for them, with constant small improvements. They were now growing into lads who helped and received a welcome from Rannulf when he saw them in Durham at the end of the day when he was in town. They got into the tradition of comparing notes with each other – a satisfying experience for all concerned.

Thomas first, then the younger boy, had nervously taken Rannulf's hand after his father received one of his numerous long-distance commissions from the king. Rannulf tried to make them as effective and as brief as possible – he no longer wanted to experience power by lingering with the King or, indeed, to be apprehended by the King himself on any grounds, real or false. But both boys realised the sympathy that lay in his gesture and the closeness that he had now come to feel as an integral part of their shared existence and to depend on it. Elias had led the way for his acknowledgement of the shrine of St Cuthbert and Bede commemorated in the chancel now finished according to his plans; certainly, both boys were appreciative of the chapel, when they first saw it and became deeply so. They had seen relatively little highly ornate decoration in England, though more commonly in Normandy, and they were deeply impressed.

The screen, especially, that had been built behind the choir to separate the area for the monks' worship from the area of the shrine itself proved magnificent. It meant that the shrine would be accessible at all times for those wishing to pay homage to St Cuthbert. The craftsmen, who had worked with the two masons during the winter, had done outstanding work, earning a huge sum too!

Shortly after Rannulf's arrival back in Durham, Turgot had been told that he had been elected to be the new Bishop of St Andrews. But religious squabbles and politics between St Andrews and the Archbishop of York delayed his ordination. It was 1109 before Turgot finally resigned his position in Durham and made the move to Scotland.

That same year Archbishop Anselm died. It was a watershed year for Rannulf. It was time to put his fractious relationship with both the church hierarchy and his Prior behind him. It was time to build a fresh partnership with the newly elected Prior of the monastery. He took the opportunity to separate the administration of his bishopric from the running of the cathedral, at the same time, making changes that would enable him to devote more time to both his pastoral duties and his civil duties, including the enormous fortification project.

With Turgot gone, the new prior was not given charge of the archdeaconry of the Palatinate of Durham; he appointed his own choice. A while later, he also created the archdeaconry of Northumberland, appointing his son by Aelgifu, Rannulf, as Archdeacon.

The plight of the poor and elderly in Durham greatly concerned Rannulf. To begin to address this, he decided to enlist the help of his more sober, elder son, Thomas. He would champion the building of a hospital for the care of the poor and unwell. It was to be called The Hospital of St Giles. The new settlement included a stone-built chapel (which later became known as St Giles Church) and several wattle and daub or wooden living spaces. The hospital was dedicated to the honour of God and St Giles, the patron saint of beggars and cripples, in a ceremony in 1112. In a charter of the time, Rannulf endowed lands, including a manor, a water mill and several sources of corn, "for the maintenance of a clerk who is to serve there and of the poor who are to be admitted". The hospital was located close to the new market area but on the opposite, eastern side of the river. In his charter, he specified that these arrangements "should perpetually remain for the salvation of his own soul, for the salvation of King William II who elevated him to the honour of the bishopric and King Henry who confirmed me in that honour and for the redemption of the souls of King William the Conqueror and Matilda his Queen who gave me promotion and the souls of those making any gift to the church of St Cuthbert."

The first person to be appointed clerk of the new hospital was Godric. Rannulf had first met Godric shortly after arriving in Durham. Godric was of similar age to Rannulf though he was born in Norfolk. He had first traded as a pedlar before eventually becoming a ship's captain and then being part owner of two ships. He took pilgrims and goods to and from the Holy Land and it was on one trip, whilst calling at Lindisfarne, that he was inspired by the work of St Cuthbert, a much earlier abbot there. He gave up his previous work to dedicate himself to helping the poor and sick. He went to Durham, where St Cuthbert was now buried. But after a while, he realised, like Cuthbert before him, that he could be more effective and closer to God if he could find a place where he could live and work as a hermit. He approached Rannulf for help and Bishop Rannulf agreed to allocate some forest land by the banks of the River Wear just a few miles outside Durham at a place called Finchale. Godric had much to learn and so was grateful that Rannulf appointed him as the first clerk at the new Hospital of St Giles. After a time, Godric established his hermitage with its own chapel and hospice at Finchale. He cared for all in need including the animals of the forest.

Rannulf persuaded Godric to take on Thomas to help him establish the hermitage and later to run the chapel and hospice. At first, he could not bear for his elder son, who had a sort of serious sobriety that he felt in need of, rather belatedly, to be separated from him either permanently or otherwise. The hermitage was but a short distance from Durham, and the thought that his elder son was nearby much of the time gave his father an underlying strength he had not previously felt before.

Added to which, there was all the attraction of St Cuthbert's shrine and its physical setting to radiate inspiration to Godric and Thomas.

As Godric aged, so Thomas took over the running of the hermitage. After he died, Godric became revered locally as a Saint though he was never canonised by the church.

However, Elias, the younger of Celestine's two sons, had made an effort to create some independence for himself. A focus for his endeavours was the gardens: the herbs and the fruit, particularly the nut trees, whose hazelnuts and cobnuts established and grew quickly. There were also, of course, the vegetables; many of these of everyday quality went with the roots to create soups and stews. But once good strains were successfully sought out and established, they were allocated to a neighbouring field outside the city and to other fields some way away. The Mediterranean herbs, however, required careful nurturing within small fences of wicker or even backed by stone protection somewhere near the deanery. Nevertheless, the herbs and their range, and their careful planting and arrangement in general, had become a source of pride to young Elias.

It was not until later in Rannulf's reign that the younger son joined his father in adding King's Norton in Northamptonshire and the benefice of the church of Horley in Oxfordshire to the church prebends in Lincoln to make a good living for Elias. His appointment to the benefice at Horley was made in the presence of the Bishop of Lincoln and the Bishop of Salisbury.

Rannulf felt a pang as he realised that the youth would not be congratulated by his Mama. Whilst the church authorities had agreed to the re-assignment of his prebends at Lincoln to Elias during Rannulf's lifetime and that they would revert to him if Elias died, he was disappointed that if he, Rannulf, died first then the prebends would not pass to Elias. Yet more evidence of the reforms that Anselm had introduced, in this case, preventing church positions and property from being passed on to the holder's nominee after death.

Rannulf regularly journeyed south to visit the capital, Winchester, or when the King sought him out to attend him in Normandy. Each time, he met up with his son, Elias, and whenever possible his former mistress, Aelgifu, now living in Huntingdon with her husband, his children and her two sons by Rannulf. Aelgifu was senior in age to Rannulf and he was more than happy to see her happy. She was not intended to be lonely and had so much kindness to give. He was very fond of her and he loved and cared for his two sons by her.

But Paradise could not last untrammelled forever!

On one of his journeys down south, with two of his horses, he was met on the Yorkshire/Lincolnshire border by the younger of his two sons, Elias, with the greeting: 'Oh, Father, what have you been doing? I can hardly move without being queried about it all and I am sure it will not stop. What can we do? And can we make it effective?'

Rannulf was surprised. 'What is all this about? What on earth is going on?'

'It's you and Christina of Markyate.'

'Well, what about it? You know she was the niece of our friend.' He paused a moment or two then continued, 'Part of the family which I often stay with on my way south ...' – he was referring to Aelgifu – 'there was a brouhaha, but it came to nothing. It should never have come to anything as it was all confected. I tried a silly game with Christina who was visiting her Aunt Aelgifu, at the same time I was there. Aelgifu took no notice but I'd had a drink or two, and Christina played a trick on me. But it was all lost as far as I was concerned and no more was thought of it.'

'But what happened?' the young man persisted.

'I suppose one might say I got my true desserts. But knowledge of it seems to have got about and magnified.' He thought a moment or two and then continued. 'You are probably familiar with my splendid episcopal ring. It attracted Christina's interest. I had asked Aelgifu if there was a key for my room and for Christina to bring it to my room, where I would let her examine the ring. Anyway, Christina had not had the three glasses of wine that I had had, and she simply brought the key and locked me in my room. Perhaps she did not trust my motives and that I might lock us both in my room! And that was that. I was playing a game with her, but it was taken with all seriousness, as was my reputation, apparently. Apart from anything else, at my age and with my paunch I could never have caught up with her anyway. It's sad what years without Celestine have done to my reputation. Yet the whole thing is quite funny and fit now only to have a laugh at me. No harm was done.'

He then added: 'But it was obviously magnified out of all proportion.'

The young man did not want to pursue the questioning further. But there was some of the fearlessness of his father in his temperament, and after a moment or two's reflection, he did ask his father about the alleged party that Rannulf had perhaps, or perhaps not, given for a papal official. Rumour had it that the official, a prestigious cleric, had been given the task of admonishing Rannulf because of the bishop persistently flaunting a conventional way of life. One way or another, the bishop was said to encourage wild behaviour. As an example, it was said he brazenly bedded the aforesaid papal official who had become drunk at the party. No bad behaviour had, in fact, occurred, but there was plenty of wine on offer. Certainly, the official's early visible collapse into a large bed was encouraged by the party. But yet again, the guest was so embarrassed that he was unable to complete the mission that he had allegedly been allocated, so nothing further was officially made public.

Rannulf hooted in derision. The whole thing smacked of a chronicler's confection and enjoyment, and it was obvious that Rannulf did not mean to take it seriously. It was also obvious that the bishop did enjoy giving parties, and there was more than one occasion when this began to be noted.

'I have done my best to keep you as remote from these as I can. But inevitably, if they don't fall on your lap, they will revert to mine. And I shall end up in the slaves' gallery! Without much means of getting out! So do go carefully!'

Whether Elias believed his father's explanations is not known, but he would undoubtedly have been aware of Rannulf's reputation for enjoying the company of women during his many years in England serving King William Rufus, living away from his family in Normandy. Some had become his mistress, or more accurately, one of his mistresses. He certainly knew about Aelgifu and her two sons by his father and he was aware of others, some of whom had borne his children. In Christina's case, history records, several years after Rannulf's death, what happened rather differently.

At the time of the incident, which Elias had quizzed him about, Christina was an attractive young woman known by her birth name of Theodora. When Rannulf met her, he was said to have lusted after her. According to one account, when Rannulf attempted to force his attentions on her, Theodora suggested she lock the door of his room to guarantee their privacy. When he agreed, she proceeded to do so but locking him in from the outside, thus trapping him in his room. Rebuffed, it is recorded that he exacted revenge by brokering a marriage for her with a young nobleman. But Christina did not accept this and ran away, taking refuge with a hermit whose cell was at Markyate sometime before 1118. It was there that she changed her name to Christina.

Perhaps this was a chronicler's 'confection' as Rannulf had suggested to his son. Theodora had pledged herself to the church from a young age but she had, for whatever reason, married this young man. Realising that she had broken her pledge, the marriage was not consummated and was later annulled by the authorities. But these events risked tarnishing her reputation within the church. So perhaps the chronicler's confection served a purpose; after all (miss-) using Rannulf's reputation was an easy sell.

Back in Durham, one of the most taxing tasks he had set himself, which plagued him for the remainder of his life, was how to manage the expectation of the continuation of the long-standing tradition of sanctuary, which had originated soon after St Cuthbert's remains were brought to Durham. He discovered first-hand how much more difficult it was to overlay or revise an established procedure on the ground than to introduce some totally novel exaction. In a way, these problems, with no completely right solution, were more intriguing than before. But they also led to moral questions: 'were his responsibilities as a royal officer, Prince Bishop, to prevail rather than his responsibility as a Bishop?' He found it almost impossible to transform himself into his new role overnight. And until he did so, opprobrium and opposition rained down on the question of Sanctuary. He himself had instigated the idea and raised the money accompanying the translation of the bones of St Cuthbert to a new splendid sanctuary that he had ordered to be built within.

Everyone had assumed that St Cuthbert's sanctuary would be available to those accused, particularly those fearing for their life. But, he asked in practice, exactly how long for? And what was to be done about a thief or suspect killer with an evil reputation? Were they to completely escape justice, and reside almost permanently at the centre of this great religious institution, alongside holy, peaceful and vulnerable monks who did nothing other than serve God?

Rannulf was one of the few Norman churchmen who had stoutly defended the traditions and rites of the English church. And the traditions of St Cuthbert were pre-eminent here. Whilst possibly killers or thieves, some of the men who stood outside the church here were villeins, or at least claimed to be so, with whom he had great sympathy, as a natural survivor, almost rebel, picked up from his time spent with his grandfather. Some would be from the bishopric's own estates, whose labour was essential to the care of their livestock and harvests. The answer was not obvious: there seemed to be no 'right' answer. As the nave was nearing completion towards the end of Rannulf's life, the way forward emerged.

The person requesting sanctuary would be seen approaching by a monk always to be stationed, day and night, in one of two small rooms located directly above the main door on the north side of the nave. Signalling intent by knocking on the door, a monk would quickly appear to let the person in. If their case proved valid, sanctuary would be offered but in a confined area. The monks would provide food and drink and guard the rights of sanctuary for up to 35 days. Sanctuary would be no easy choice; life would be difficult but safe providing breathing space for the applicant to make his own decision. They could hope to prove their innocence, decide to face justice or accept being banished forever from the diocese. After 35 days they would leave.

The original knocker, shown below, is now kept in the safety of the Cathedral collections though a replica is still mounted on the door.

After Archbishop Anselm's death in 1109 and the antagonism now gone, Rannulf's standing within the church grew each year as did his relationship with the King. Henry had summoned Rannulf to accompany him to Normandy on several occasions in 1115 and 1118-19 to advise him on financial matters. But the king did not have the camaraderie and humour given him by his previous two Royal superiors, William Rufus and even Duke Robert of Normandy. Rannulf preferred to keep Henry at arm's length.

As Prince Bishop, Rannulf had decided not to press Henry to formally give him the many powers typically held by a Prince Bishop, though he did assume the power of appointing a sheriff to enforce the collection of dues in Northumberland. He appointed his nephew, Osbert, Sheriff of Northumberland. He insisted on establishing his own hunting rights in his forest land, completely independent of the much-disliked Forest Law established by the Conqueror elsewhere in England; he wanted freedom to enjoy his favourite pastime. But Rannulf's priority was to ensure none of his work in Durham could be obliterated by a speedy Scottish siege, or should be held even longer by a more devastating occupation. In these matters, Rannulf's and Henry's needs were therefore aligned and he was able this way to keep Henry out of his business

Once Rannulf's work to secure the boundaries of the peninsular was completed, he turned his attention to securing the most northerly border of his extensive lands which included an outlier manor called Norham, strategically placed on the River Tweed, the border with Scotland. The risk of invasion by the Scots was the highest threat to the security of both his county and to England. Rannulf commissioned the building of Norham Castle in 1121.

Rannulf's vision for protecting the Palatinate of Durham was not only implemented in his lifetime but stood the test of time; Durham was not invaded again. Rannulf relished the challenge of forever needing to balance the demands of skilled labour to building these civil works and completing the cathedral. Work on completing the cathedral now accelerated but sadly Rannulf's time on Earth was coming to an end in 1128.

Chapter 8

The End

Realising he was nearing his end on Earth, Rannulf decided to formalise the verbal pledge that his predecessor, William St Calais, had made with the monks of the monastery in 1093. In early August, Rannulf signed a charter "restoring to St Cuthbert and his monks everything that he took from them on his accession to the see, including altar offerings and income from the church burials, and the land beyond the bridge of Durham and other places". The charter was signed and sealed in early August 1128.

Come early September, Rannulf lay on his trestle getting weaker each day. He hoped he was near the end; above all he hated his inactivity and his uselessness, his consumption of the time of others, even of his own time, wasted with the offers of bodily comfort and herbal release. He needed a time of quiet and thought before his mind or his consciousness failed him, to begin to make his peace with those of his past life whom he had perhaps wronged.

'Father, forgive me. I have always tried my utmost to live up to your precepts, and to my conscience.' He could not avoid adding 'and my own loves, and needs' and added 'implanted in me by you from my long experience of your own tender love.'

One of those near him, bent close to hear his mutterings, in case they were instructions about the community, prayers for the dying man, or bequests in perpetuity. The monk drew back a little when he realised that Rannulf was confessing to his Maker, in a subdued, but private, not public, tone.

Fortunately, the monk did not comprehend that the image that flickered in and out of Rannulf's failing vision was that of his own father. Rannulf had long merged the image of his own father with that of God the Father; with his own direct knowledge of the deity almost entirely framed by the example of his earthly father and the precepts and texts taught by him. It was to his earthly father's standards he made practical reference, even if he prayed to God the Father in the services in the cathedral.

When he was younger and first realised that he was apt to do this, he reflected on the practice long and hard. But in his common-sense way, he realised, at least to his own satisfaction, that the standards of conduct of his own earthly father fulfilled the beatitudes rather better than most of the most learned and the spiritual fathers of the church. And if he felt he needed help visualising God the Father, then his own father, his conduct and sentiments, remained the highest earthly standard that he could visualise.

'Father, I endeavoured in dangerous times always to keep my promise to look after you, my mother and my brothers and sister. The need for some good position then led me further than I intended into worldly concerns. Once on this path, it became a treadmill. I also saw that my own peculiar skills and qualities were needed to prevent further warfare and civil war. Or at least try to. I made mistakes … of course I did … great mistakes, but they were seldom the mistakes for which I was punished by king, dukes or archbishop. Nor those I have been pilloried for by the chroniclers in the monasteries. Probably my greatest sins were to my own loves and families and my own needs to replace a loving close family. I always tried to look after them as best I could: I should have so much more loved to spend time with them – my little sons became lost to me in Normandy. Again, I spent too much time with higher politics and the Duke Robert's concerns, partly so that they should have a secure future.'

The aroma of the herbs spread around his room, lulled him deeper into dreamland. He remembered his parents' herb garden at home in Bayeux and his own family's herb garden in Lisieux and his grandfather's gardens and crop lands that he had visited many times. He appreciated the peace these places gave him and realised their value in health, making of ale, and good eating. He had enjoyed introducing some of these to the gardens and fields in Durham. The pleasure that his two young sons gave him when they rose to the challenge of helping the monks of his beloved monastery improve and extend the gardens of the monastery, both near the kitchen and the hospital, thrilled him. He thanked his mother and his wife for nurturing these skills and their love of horses in the two lads and he realised that it was the gardens and the stables of the peninsular which had allowed the bond with his sons to belatedly develop.

He had been able to instill the same values that his parents and grandparents had instilled in him into his sons. But he had also come to realise in those early days back in Durham that he needed to let them carve out their own futures with just a soft touch on the tiller from him, just as his own father had done, to guide them on their way. He remembered after his escape from the Tower, his mother and Celest had both pleaded with him to devote more time to his young family. But he had been unable to resist capturing the bishopric of Lisieux by pushing forward his young son Thomas, with the grateful Duke Robert's blessing, into that role; both sons hated it and they were ill-suited for it. It was probably this act of selfishness which contributed to their poor health and ultimately the untimely death of his beloved wife. He thought of Celestine often. It drove him into fits of melancholy caused by the guilt he had for not supporting her when she needed it and for realising the intense love he had for her only when it was too late.

It seemed as though his loss of Celestine, just when a new life beckoned for all of them, was what had inspired him and motivated him to devote the rest of life not only to raising his sons but to complete the building of the cathedral, supporting the monastery, and turning the peninsular into a safe and secure place for the monks and all those who supported the work and life of the bishopric, not just in Durham but throughout the Palatinate.

His mother, as long as she had lived, had been remarkable in providing for him in many practical ways. Oh, he did thank his God that his mother had been so active and long-lived: that surely was God-sent. Without her, his own children would have lacked her all-round embracing care and he would have lacked her vigilance in connecting him with their needs. He desperately wanted his mother to accompany them to Durham. He remembered weeping when she told him, 'I'm sorry, Rannulf. I can't cope with the journeys by ship across the Channel any more. I've done my best and loved the opportunity to see the world a little; I should like to support you, especially now our lovely Celestine cannot rise to that challenge, but have now got rather too old and doddery to cope with both Durham and Normandy. And, of course, I too, sadly have now lost your father.'

He recalled the joy in his soul at the way the sanctuary for the Venerable Bede and St Cuthbert had become fulfilled. He was always aware that his sons shared that sense of rejoicing.

He knew that he was often thought of by outsiders as avaricious, greedy. According to appearances by some he never ceased to accumulate riches, yet eventually they would see them devoted only to the purchase of foreign wine and to the sweetest wines which could be made at home from lemon balm, lavender, parsnips, or sweet marjoram, and which his officials as well as the monks could take and sample on occasions of mutual rejoicing. Otherwise, his revenues were dedicated to the church buildings and to secure his position and the assets he was creating for the young monks.

Curiously, he remembered the payment of one thousand pounds he had made to and had been accepted by the King shortly after Henry came to power. He knew that it was much talked about behind his back and not in kindly ways. Everyone knew that such payments were not unusual in those times as would be bishops sought the nomination of the monarch. But in his case, the King had not demanded it, rather he, Rannulf, had volunteered it, realising that he remained vulnerable to being the escaped prisoner, still not forgiven, not pardoned. It was a small price to pay for making his own position as a free man and Prince Bishop of Durham more secure on a formal footing.

Although he had enjoyed his work for the King during Rufus' reign, he acknowledged that he had made many enemies by his actions, particularly in the church and with the landed barons. Although what he had done was not illegal, his actions were at the edge of legality relying on the powers and instruction of the King. He did realise that his action, his idea, of raising money from the fyrd was a step too far and the demanding of money from the tenants of the Bishop of Worcester to retain, or effectively buy back, the tenancies they held of the bishop at his death, was certainly a step too far. Such lands were held by the Bishopric, not the Bishop, and therefore not even subject to the customary 'fines' paid on the death of the lord, and certainly not the King! He had not repeated these actions but he knew he had damaged his reputation. But in all this work, he had never sought to extend these practices to the less well off; his grandfather had taught him well.

He looked back on the many projects that he oversaw on Rufus' behalf – the Tower of London walls, Westminster Hall, the stone bridge over the Thames and the projects he had personally initiated such as the rebuilding of Christchurch Priory – with much satisfaction. He had learned important skills during his service to Rufus that had enabled him to undertake his massive projects in Durham. He took comfort that King Henry, despite having made shameful and derisive betrayal of all his hard work for Henry's brother Rufus and of his own father, had, in the cool light of day, secure in his throne, been pleased to allow him back to his bishopric and to maintain the health and welfare of his English family.

He gave thanks, too, for having been given the opportunity to serve William, The Conqueror. He knew that it was his wife, Queen Matilda, who had recommended him after his mentor, Odo, had been imprisoned shortly after returning from his expedition to Durham. His selection to work on Domesday had taught him much and enabled him to make many contacts that would be important to him during his later years.

Although his reputation for enjoying life during this time was an open secret, his many mistresses in England were more discreet. He had several children by these women, but he always recognised his obligations and made sure he provided for them. His relationship with Aelfigu was special. She was special. He knew he could not continue his ways with her after his appointment as Bishop in 1099 and was happy for her and her sons that he was able to have her married to a burgess in Huntingdon. He had maintained friendly relations with both her and her husband, always providing for those children, and when he could, stopped by to visit them in Huntingdon when he was travelling to or from the south.

Among his most cherished memories of those early formative years, was of his trusty palomino mare and his time spent in the cathedral stables. That first journey on horseback to visit his grandfather under the guidance of Bran was forever etched in his memory. It had given him confidence and had led him into his own almost private world in the stables where he first encountered and then trained the palomino before leaving for Durham with Odo's forces. Many times they had zig-zagged across England during his work on Domesday and later on his visits to the monasteries temporarily under his care. He wanted her to enjoy her last years in Durham and be in the company of the new mares that he had trained in Lisieux and then brought back to Durham. Blessed times.

But it was his close family he most mourned; his father, mother, grandfather, his sons, and Celestine.

Rannulf died that evening: September 5, 1128. He was buried under the floor of the monastery's Chapter House in keeping with the promise to keep the chancel of the cathedral sacred to the memory only of St Cuthbert and the Venerable Bede. The Chapter House, originally built by Bishop Walcher as a meeting room for the canons of the Anglo-Saxon collegiate church, which was demolished by Bishop St Calais before construction of the cathedral started in 1094, was already the burial site of Bishop Walcher and Bishop St Calais. The cathedral was completed in 1132 and consecrated in 1133 when Rannulf's successor was also consecrated.

Despite the many changes made to the Chapter House over the centuries, the building remains their final resting place. Seven stained glass windows were installed in 1935, three of which honour the contributions of Walcher, St Calais, and Rannulf. The three windows are shown in the photograph below on page 143; that commemorating Rannulf is on the right.

One of the monks of Durham, who had known both Rannulf and Godric, and who had chronicled the life of St Godric just a few decades later, wrote of Rannulf: 'That was our golden age, under Rannulf our Bishop'. From one who knew him, his impressive reputation was 'impatient of leisure, he went on from labour to labour, thinking nothing done unless new enterprises pressed on the heels of those already accomplished'.

References and further reading

Sally Harvey: *Domesday, Book of Judgement* from Oxford University Press, published 2014

R W Southern: *Ranulf Flambard and Early Anglo-Norman Administration*, The Alexander Prize Essay, published by Cambridge University Press 1933

Jones, Fowler and Thorpe: *Bishop Flambard's Great Wall at Durham*, published 1916, from Durham Cathedral Library

H S Offler: *Rannulf Flambard as Bishop of Durham, !913 Cathedral Lecture*, from Durham Cathedral Library

www.durhamworldheritagesite.com   Check on the 'Learn' tab

Wikipedia for names, places , events, Norman law and customs and much more.

About the Authors

Although retired from academia for ten years, Sally preferred to write this book under her professional name, her maiden name, Dr Sally Harvey. Sally was an academic historian specialising in the Norman Conquest and Domesday. Over her fifty-year career, she lectured and researched at the Universities of Oxford, Leeds and Cambridge and, in 2014, published her much-praised book, *Domesday, Book of Judgement*. In one of the chapters, The Mastermind, she documents her research into the six most likely candidates who might have been the architect of Domesday. Rannulf Flambard's case is written at length and illustrates the depth to which she worked to understand this remarkable man. It is perhaps no surprise that, in her retirement, she decided to write about Rannulf, someone she greatly admired, someone who was rarely described in good terms by the Chroniclers of Medieval times, yet who achieved so much of lasting importance to England. Sally married Leslie Fielding, later knighted for his services to diplomacy, in 1978. Lady Fielding now lives in Malvern.

Gordon Sawyer worked for the oil industry giant ExxonMobil for forty years before retiring in 2003. He and his wife Sue had already developed a passion for family history research. So, when they moved to the historic town of Arundel, perhaps it was no surprise that his interest in history grew. He became a Trustee of the Arundel Museum Society before moving to Strensham in Worcestershire where he decided to research the history of this quiet rural parish. He published his findings in his first book, *The Ancient Manor of Strensham* in 2020. Gordon and Sue moved to Malvern in 2022, there becoming a neighbour and friend of Lady Fielding.

www.ingramcontent.com/pod-product-compliance
Lightning Source LLC
Chambersburg PA
CBHW041144110526
44590CB00027B/4116